Frommer's®

New York City
day BY day

4th Edition

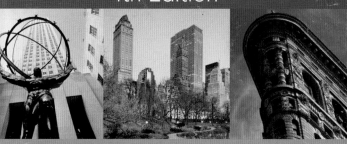

by Brian Silverman

FrommerMedia LLC

Contents

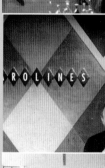

Published by:

Frommer Media LLC

ISBN: 978-1-628-87021-3 (paper); ISBN 978-1-628-87051-0 (ebk)

Editorial Director: Pauline Frommer
Editor: Kate Hambrecht
Production Editor: Heather Wilcox
Photo Editor: Seth Olenick
Cartographer: Roberta Stockwell
Page Compositor: Heather Pope
Indexer: Cheryl Lenser

For information on our other products and services, please go to Frommers.com.

Frommer's also publishes its books in a variety of electronic formats. Some content that appears in print may not be available in electronic formats.

Manufactured in China

5   4   3   2   1

About This Book

Organizing your time. That's what this guide is all about.

Other guides give you long lists of things to see and do and then expect you to fit the pieces together. The Day by Day guides are different. These guides tell you the best of everything, and then they show you how to see it in the smartest, most time-efficient way. Our authors have designed detailed itineraries organized by time, neighborhood, or special interest. And each tour comes with a bulleted map that takes you from stop to stop.

Whatever your interest or schedule, the Day by Days give you the smartest routes to follow. Not only do we take you to the top attractions, hotels, and restaurants, but we also help you access those special moments that locals get to experience—those "finds" that turn tourists into travelers.

The Day by Days are also your top choice if you're looking for one complete guide for all your travel needs. The best hotels and restaurants for every budget, the greatest shopping values, the wildest nightlife—it's all here.

Why should you trust our judgment? Because our authors personally visit each place they write about. They're an independent lot who say what they think and would never include places they wouldn't recommend to their best friends. They're also open to suggestions from readers. If you'd like to contact them, please send your comments our way at Support@FrommerMedia.com, and we'll pass them on.

Enjoy your Day by Day guide—the most helpful travel companion you can buy. And have the trip of a lifetime.

About the Author

The author of more than 15 *Frommer's New York City* guide books, **Brian Silverman's** writings on food and travel have been published in such magazines as *Saveur, The New Yorker, Caribbean Travel & Life, Islands, Four Seasons*. He is also the author of numerous books, including *Going, Going, Gone: History, Lore and Mystique of the Home Run* and *The Twentieth Century Treasury of Sports*. He is also the creator of the website *Fried Neck Bones . . . and Some Home Fries* at www.fried neckbonesandsomehomefries.com. He lives in New York with his wife and two children.

An Additional Note

Please be advised that travel information is subject to change at any time—and this is especially true of prices. We therefore suggest that you write or call ahead for confirmation when making your travel plans. The authors, editors, and publisher cannot be held responsible for the experiences of readers while traveling. Your safety is important to us, however, so we encourage you to stay alert and be aware of your surroundings.

Star Ratings, Icons & Abbreviations

Every hotel, restaurant, and attraction listing in this guide has been ranked for quality, value, service, amenities, and special features using a **star-rating system.** Hotels, restaurants, attractions, shopping, and nightlife are rated on a scale of zero stars (recommended) to three stars (exceptional). In addition to the star-rating system, we also use a **kids icon** to point out the best bets for families. Within each tour, we recommend cafes, bars, or restaurants where you can take a break. Each of these stops appears in a shaded box marked with a coffee-cup-shaped bullet 🍵.

The following **abbreviations** are used for credit cards:

AE	American Express	DISC	Discover	V	Visa
DC	Diners Club	MC	MasterCard		

Travel Resources at Frommers.com

Frommer's travel resources don't end with this guide. Frommer's website, **www.frommers.com**, has travel information on more than 4,000 destinations. We update features regularly, giving you access to the most current trip-planning information and the best airfare, lodging, and car-rental bargains. You can also listen to podcasts, connect with other Frommers.com members through our active-reader forums, share your travel photos, read blogs from guidebook editors and fellow travelers, and much more.

A Note on Prices

In the "Take a Break" and "Best Bets" sections of this book, we have used a system of dollar signs to show a range of costs for 1 night in a hotel (the price of a double-occupancy room) or the cost of an entree at a restaurant. Use the following table to decipher the dollar signs:

Cost	Hotels	Restaurants
$	under $130	under $15
$$	$130–$200	$15–$30
$$$	$200–$300	$30–$40
$$$$	$300–$395	$40–$50
$$$$$	over $395	over $50

How to Contact Us

In researching this book, we discovered many wonderful places—hotels, restaurants, shops, and more. We're sure you'll find others. Please tell us about them, so we can share the information with your fellow travelers in upcoming editions. If you were disappointed with a recommendation, we'd love to know that, too. Please write to: Support@FrommerMedia.com

15 Favorite
Moments

15 Favorite Moments

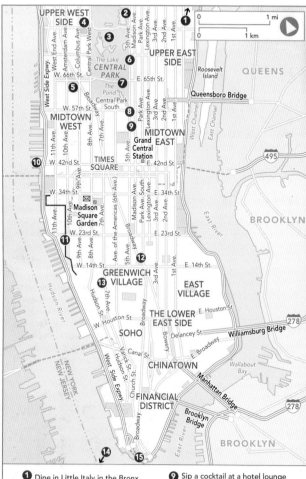

1. Dine in Little Italy in the Bronx
2. Say hello to Rembrandt at the Met
3. Play in Central Park
4. Stare up at the *Barosaurus*
5. Dress up for the opera
6. Feel like a Gilded Age millionaire
7. Visit Gus the polar bear at the Central Park Zoo
8. Window-shop on Fifth Avenue
9. Sip a cocktail at a hotel lounge
10. See Manhattan on a sunset cruise
11. Promenade along the High Line
12. Get a taste of the Greenmarket in Union Square
13. Comb the storied streets of Greenwich Village
14. Climb to Lady Liberty's Crown
15. Smell the sea at Battery Park

Previous page: The Manhattan skyline, as seen from Brooklyn and the Brooklyn Bridge.

Visitors often wonder how Manhattan residents put up with the city's crowds and frenetic pace—not to mention the tiny, cramped apartments. But when I'm out exploring any of the 15 attractions below, I wouldn't be anywhere else. Every New Yorker has a list of favorite places to visit and things to see. Here's mine.

1 Dine in Little Italy in the Bronx. Stroll down Arthur Avenue or Belmont Avenue and window-shop the bakeries, cheese shops, and meat purveyors. Then order a big red-sauce-laden meal in one of the neighborhood's old-fashioned Italian restaurants. My pick? The legendary Dominick's. *See p 118.*

2 Say hello to Rembrandt at the Met. A self-portrait of the Dutch painter is one of thousands of masterpieces on view at the Metropolitan Museum of Art, the city's premier museum and one of the world's best. It's open until 9pm on Friday and Saturday nights, so soak up a little art and sip an evening cocktail at the elegant Great Hall Balcony Bar, or on the Roof Garden if it's warm out. *See p 46.*

3 Play in Central Park. Manhattan's backyard is loved for its endless variety: undulating paths and greenswards, formal gardens, boat ponds, a castle, a puppet theater, an Egyptian obelisk, a lake, and even a storied carousel. *See p 104.*

4 Stare up at the *Barosaurus.* Yes, the largest freestanding mounted dinosaur in the world is impressive, but the American Museum of Natural History offers more than just giant reptile fossils. The adjacent Rose Center/Hayden Planetarium is spectacular during the day—and pure magic at night. *See p 54.*

5 Dress up for the opera. Even on casual Fridays, New Yorkers like to get gussied up to see Metropolitan Opera productions at Lincoln Center. (The sets alone are reason to visit.) Opera not your bag? Simply cross the renovated plaza to see world-class performances in ballet, the symphony, and theater. *See p 140.*

6 Feel like a Gilded Age millionaire. Take a walk in a robber baron's slippers and see priceless art in the bargain at steel magnate Henry Frick's Fifth Avenue mansion. The warm, elegant rooms are hung with choice works by Rembrandt, El Greco, Gainsborough, and other masters. *See p 25.*

7 Visit Gus the polar bear at the Central Park Zoo. This small-scale zoo is perfect for kids and adults in need of a relaxing break from big-city prowling. The animals at play include polar bears, penguins, monkeys, and a shy snow leopard. *See p 30.*

The Gramercy Hotel's Jade Bar.

8 Window-shop on Fifth Avenue.
Legendary stores, such as Saks,
Bergdorf Goodman, Tiffany & Co.,
Cartier, and Harry Winston, rub
shoulders with va-va-va-voom
upstarts, such as Gucci, Cavalli, and
Versace—with each vying equally
hard for attention, it's hard to
choose. See p 100.

9 Sip a cocktail at a hotel lounge.
Choose an old standard, such as
Bemelman's Bar in the Carlyle or
the King Cole Lounge in the St.
Regis. Or sample classics in the
making, such as the Gramercy
Hotel's Rose Bar or Jade Bar or the
Jimmy on the rooftop of the James
Hotel. See p 131.

**10 See Manhattan on a sunset
cruise.** The city that never sleeps
begins to glitter at dusk, when millions of lights set it aglow. Take a
sunset cruise on the mighty Hudson
for wraparound views of the city
skyline and its splendid evening
sparkle. See p 18.

*New York, and the Empire State Building,
at dusk.*

**11 Promenade along the High
Line.** The High Line has become
one of the city's must-sees. The
reinvention of an elevated freight-
train track into a series of innovative outdoor habitats is inspired.
Your meditative *passeggiata*
above the urban din includes
sweeping Hudson River vistas.
See p 110.

**12 Get a taste of the Greenmar-
ket in Union Square.** Country
comes to city 4 days a week year-
round at New York's largest farmer's market. The excellent fresh
flowers, produce, meats, and other
artisanal food are grown by small
farmers on Long Island and in New
Jersey. Open Monday, Wednesday,
Friday, and Saturday. See p 99.

**13 Comb the storied streets of
Greenwich Village.** This historic,
human-scale neighborhood affords
serendipitous charms around every
corner—from vintage brownstones
to fabled watering holes. Many
famous writers, artists, and poets of
yesteryear called this former hamlet
home. See p 76.

14 Climb to Lady Liberty's crown.
When was the last time someone
gave you a 151-foot copper statue
to express their admiration? In
1886, France gave the U.S. the
beloved Statue of Liberty; if you
can climb the 354 steps to her
crown, you'll be treated to a view
of New York Harbor that has been
thrilling generations ever since.
See p 17.

15 Smell the sea at Battery Park.
This is where Manhattan was born.
Start at the yacht basin at the
World Financial Center and head
south. When you reach the southern tip of Manhattan, you get a
magnificent view of the mouth
of the mighty New York Harbor
with ships chugging into view.
See p 17. ●

1

The Best
Full-Day Tours

The Best **in One Day**

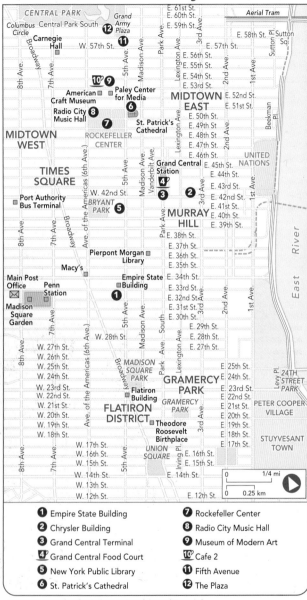

- ❶ Empire State Building
- ❷ Chrysler Building
- ❸ Grand Central Terminal
- ❹ Grand Central Food Court
- ❺ New York Public Library
- ❻ St. Patrick's Cathedral
- ❼ Rockefeller Center
- ❽ Radio City Music Hall
- ❾ Museum of Modern Art
- ❿ Cafe 2
- ⓫ Fifth Avenue
- ⓬ The Plaza

Previous page: The Sky Ceiling at Grand Central Terminal.

The most wonderful—and maddening—thing about New York? The endless number of choices. Start your urban exploration in Midtown, the city's business and commercial heart. Yes, the shopping opportunities here are legion, and the air space is dotted with corporate skyscrapers—but Midtown is also home to several quintessential New York landmarks. START: **Subway 6 to 33rd Street or B, D, F, M, N, Q, or R to 34th Street.**

❶ ★★ Empire State Building.

King Kong climbed it in 1933. A plane slammed into it in 1945. After September 11, 2001, the Empire State regained its status as New York City's tallest building. Through it all, it has remained one of the city's favorite landmarks. Completed in 1931, the limestone-and-stainless-steel Art Deco dazzler climbs 103 stories (1,454 ft./436m). The best views are from the 86th- and 102nd-floor observatories, but I prefer the former, from which you can walk onto an outer windswept deck. From here, the citywide panorama is electric. Lines can be long on weekends. ⏱ *2 hr. 350 Fifth Ave. (at 34th St.).* ☎ *212/736-3100. www.esbnyc.com. Observatory admission (86th floor) $25 adults, $22 seniors, $19 children 6–12, free for children 5 & under. ESB Express pass: $47.50. 102nd floor observatory: $15 extra. Observatories open daily 8am–2am; last elevator goes up at 1:15am. Subway: 6 to 33rd St.; B/D/F/M to 34th St.*

❷ ★★★ Chrysler Building.

Built as the Chrysler Corporation headquarters in 1930, this is New York's most romantic Art Deco masterpiece and, for many New Yorkers, its most endearing visual touchstone. It's especially dramatic at night, when the triangular points in its steely crown are outlined in silvery lights. The marble-clad lobby is a hymn to Deco; a mural on the ceiling was actually rediscovered in 1999. *See p 177.*

❸ ★★ Grand Central Terminal.

An iconic Beaux Arts beauty. The highlight is the vast, imposing main concourse, where high windows allow sunlight to pour onto the half-acre (.25-ha) Tennessee-marble floor. Everything gleams, from the brass clock over the central kiosk to the gold- and nickel-plated chandeliers piercing the side archways. The breathtaking **Sky Ceiling** depicts the constellations of the winter sky above New York. *42nd St. & Park Ave.* ☎ *212/340-2210. www.grandcentralterminal. com. Subway: 4/5/6/7/S to 42nd St.*

Gargoyles perched high on the Chrysler Building.

4 ★ **Grand Central Food Court.** We're at Grand Central already, so head down to the lower-level food court. From New York cheesecake (Junior's) to top-notch soup (Hale & Hearty), Indian (Spice), pizza (Two Boots), and, of course, seafood at the famous Oyster Bar, the choices are delicious and fast, and the seating plentiful. $–$$.

5 ★ **New York Public Library.** The lions *Patience* and *Fortitude* stand guard outside the grand Fifth Avenue entrance of the **Main Branch (Stephen A. Schwarzman Building)** of the public library, designed by Carrère & Hastings in 1911. It's one of the country's finest examples of Beaux Arts architecture. Sadly, architect John Mervin Carrère never got to enjoy the fruits of his labor; he was killed in a taxi accident 2 months before the library dedication. The majestic white-marble structure is filled with Corinthian columns and allegorical statues. The original Winnie the Pooh stuffed bear is on display in the children's Center. ⏱ *1 hr. Fifth Ave. (btw. 42nd & 40th sts.).* ☎ *917/275-6975. www.nypl.org. Free admission. Mon & Thurs–Sat 10am–6pm, Tues–Wed 10am–8pm, Sun 1–5pm. Subway: B/D/F/M to 42nd St.*

6 ★★ **St. Patrick's Cathedral.** This Gothic white-marble-and-stone wonder is the largest Roman Catholic cathedral in the U.S. Designed by James Renwick, begun in 1859, and

Marble lions guard the New York Public Library.

consecrated in 1879, St. Patrick's wasn't completed until 1906. You can pop in between services to get a look at the impressive interior. The St. Michael and St. Louis altar came from Tiffany & Co., while the St. Elizabeth altar—honoring Mother Elizabeth Ann Seton, the first American-born saint—was designed by Paolo Medici of Rome. ⏱ *15 min. Fifth Ave. (btw. 50th & 51st sts.).* ☎ *212/753-2261. www. saintpatrickscathedral.org. Free admission. Daily 6:30am–8:45pm. Subway: B/D/F/M to 47th–50th sts./ Rockefeller Center.*

7 ★★★ **Rockefeller Center.** A prime example of civic optimism expressed in soaring architecture, Rock Center was built in the 1930s. Designated a National Historic Landmark in 1988, it's now the world's largest privately owned business-and-entertainment center, with 18 buildings on 21 acres. The **GE Building,** also known as **30 Rock,** at 30 Rockefeller Plaza, is a 70-story showpiece; walk through the granite-and-marble lobby lined with handsome murals by Spanish painter José Maria Sert (1874–1945). The mammoth Rockefeller Christmas tree is placed in the plaza fronting 30 Rock, overlooking the famous skating rink. *Bounded by 48th & 51st sts. & Fifth & Sixth aves. Subway: B/D/F/M to 47th–50th sts./ Rockefeller Center.*

8 ★★★ **Radio City Music Hall.** Designed by Donald Deskey and opened in 1932, this sumptuous Art Deco classic is the world's largest indoor theater, with 6,000 seats. Long known for its Rockettes revues and

The Palm Court at the Plaza.

popular Christmas show, Radio City also has a stellar history as a venue for movie premieres. (More than 700 films have opened here since 1933.) The Deco "powder rooms" are some of the swankiest in town. *1260 Sixth Ave. (at 50th St.).* ☎ *212/247-4777. www.radiocity. com. 1-hr. Stage Door Tour daily 11am–3pm (extended hours Nov 15– Dec 30). Tickets $23 adults, $18 seniors, $16 children 12 & under. Subway: B/D/F/M to 47th–50th sts./ Rockefeller Center.*

⑨ ★★★ Museum of Modern Art. MoMA houses the world's greatest collection of painting and sculpture from the late 19th century to the present—from Monet's Water Lilies and Klimt's The Kiss to 20th-century masterworks by Frida Kahlo and Jasper Johns to contemporary pieces by Richard Serra and Chuck Close. Add to that a vast collection of modern drawings, photos, architectural models and modern furniture, iconic design objects ranging from tableware to sports cars, and film and video. ⏱ *3 hr. See p 56.*

⑩ ★★ Fifth Avenue. New York's most famous shopping artery starts at the southeast corner of Central Park at 59th Street. Some landmarks to note: **FAO Schwarz,** at no. 767 (58th St.), the city's top toy emporium; **Tiffany & Co.,** at no. 727 (btw. 56th & 57th sts.), with its stainless-steel doors and Atlas clock; gilded **Trump Tower,** at no. 725 (56th St.), with a seven-story waterfall; **Henri Bendel,** at no. 712 (btw. 55th & 56th sts.), a whimsical department store with vintage Lalique art-glass windows; and **Bergdorf Goodman** at 754 (at 57th St.). *Subway: N/R/W to Fifth Ave./59th St.*

⑪ ★ The Plaza. There's no denying the glamour of the Big Apple's most famous hotel (which is divided between hotel rooms and private condos, with restaurants and shops on the ground floor). This 1907 landmark French Renaissance palace has hosted royalty, celebrities, and a legion of honeymooners. Have afternoon tea in the legendary **Palm Court** or sip a cup of coffee in the **Champagne Bar.** *768 Fifth Ave. (at Central Park South).* ☎ *888/850-0909. www.fairmont.com/theplaza. Subway: N/R/W to Fifth Ave./59th St.*

The Best **in Two Days**

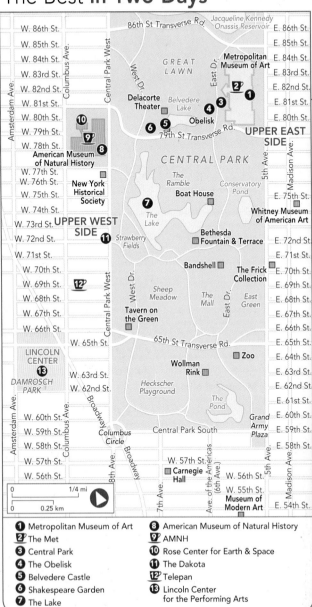

1. Metropolitan Museum of Art
2. The Met
3. Central Park
4. The Obelisk
5. Belvedere Castle
6. Shakespeare Garden
7. The Lake
8. American Museum of Natural History
9. AMNH
10. Rose Center for Earth & Space
11. The Dakota
12. Telepan
13. Lincoln Center for the Performing Arts

After the 1-day tour of Midtown, head uptown to Manhattan's artistic soul—the Metropolitan Museum and Lincoln Center. The area is also home to Central Park, an urban oasis that recharges body and mind. This part of town has a wealth of museums—most of them along Fifth Avenue. To avoid burnout, don't try to see them all in 1 day. If you have kids in tow, run, don't walk, to the American Museum of Natural History. START: **Subway 4, 5, or 6 to 86th Street.**

❶ ★★★ kids Metropolitan Museum of Art. At 1.6 million sq. ft. (148,644 sq. m), this is the largest museum in the Western Hemisphere, attracting five million visitors annually. Nearly all the world's cultures through the ages are on display—from Egyptian mummies to ancient Greek statuary to Islamic carvings to Renaissance paintings to 20th-century decorative arts—and masterpieces are the rule. You could go once a week for a lifetime and still find something new on each visit. Everyone should see the **Temple of Dendur,** the jewel of the Egyptian collection. But let personal preference be your guide to the rest. Touchstones include the exceptional Rembrandts, Vermeers, and other Dutch master painters. Transplanted period rooms—from the elegant 18th-century bedroom from a Venetian castle to the warm and inviting 20th-century Frank Lloyd Wright living room—are equally unmissable. ⏱ *3 hr. See p 46.*

❷ The Met. Eating at the Met gives you options: If you're visiting between May and October, check out the Roof Garden Café and Martini Bar ($) for breathtaking treetop views of Central Park. Year-round you can grab lunch at the ground-floor cafeteria ($), the American Wing Café ($$), or at the elegant Petrie Court Café ($$), which overlooks Central Park. On Friday and Saturday evenings, cocktails and appetizers are served at the Great Hall Balcony Bar ($) overlooking the Great Hall. *The Met, Fifth Ave. (at 82nd St.).* ☎ *212/535-7710. www. metmuseum.org.*

The Temple of Dendur at the Metropolitan Museum of Art.

3 ★★★ kids **Central Park.**
Manhattanites may lack yards, but they do have this glorious swath of green. Designed by Frederick Law Olmstead and Calvert Vaux in the 1850s, the park is 2½ miles (4km) long (extending from 59th to 110th sts.) and a half-mile (.8km) wide (from Fifth Ave. to Central Park West). It encompasses a zoo, a carousel, two ice-skating rinks (in season), restaurants, children's playgrounds, and even theaters. *See p 104.*

4 **The Obelisk.** Also called Cleopatra's Needle, this 71-ft. (21m) obelisk is reached by following the path leading west behind the Met. Originally erected in Heliopolis, Egypt, around 1475 B.C., it was given to New York by the khedive of Egypt in 1880. Continue on the path to Central Park's **Great Lawn** (p 105), site of countless softball games, concerts, and peaceful political protests.

The T. Rex at the American Museum of Natural History.

5 ★ **Belvedere Castle.** Built by Calvert Vaux in 1869, this fanciful medieval-style fortress-in-miniature sits at the highest point in Central Park and affords sweeping views. The many birds that call this area home led to the creation of a bird-watching and educational center in the castle's ranger station. To get here, follow the path across East Drive and walk west.

6 **Shakespeare Garden.** Next to Belvedere Castle, this garden grows only those flowers and plants mentioned in the Bard's plays.

7 ★★ **The Lake.** South of the garden, you'll cross the 79th Street Transverse Road to reach the Lake, with its perimeter pathway lined with weeping willows and Japanese cherry trees. The neo-Victorian **Loeb Boathouse** (p 106) at the east end of the Lake rents rowboats and bicycles; on summer evenings, you can arrange gondola rides. Walk back up to the 79th Street Transverse Road and follow it west; it exits the park at 81st Street and Central Park West. *See p 106.*

8 ★★★ kids **American Museum of Natural History.** The spectacular entrance—featuring a *Barosaurus* skeleton, the world's largest freestanding dinosaur exhibit—is just the tip of the iceberg. Founded in 1869, the AMNH houses the world's greatest natural-science collection in a square-block group of buildings made of whimsical towers and turrets, pink granite, and red brick. The diversity of the holdings is astounding: some 36 million specimens, ranging from microscopic organisms to the world's largest cut gem, the **Brazilian Princess Topaz** (21,005 carats). If you only see one exhibit, make it the ★ **dinosaurs,** which take up the entire fourth floor. *Note:* The admission lines can be tedious for young kids. If you buy advance tickets online, you can avoid the 20-minute wait. ⏱ *2 hr. See p 54.*

9 kids **AMNH.** The AMNH has a wide selection of food choices, starting with the Food Court ($), which has a kid-friendly selection of pizzas, hot entrees, sandwiches—even sushi rolls. Café on One ($) has adult-friendly paninis, salads, and lattes. The Starlight Café ($) features wraps, sandwiches, chicken nuggets, hot dogs, and fruit cups or freshly baked cookies. *American Museum of Natural History, Central Park West (btw. 77th & 81st sts.).* ☎ *212/769-5100. www.amnh.org.*

The dome of the Hayden Planetarium, at the Rose Center for Earth & Space.

10 ★★ kids **Rose Center for Earth & Space.** Attached to the American Museum of Natural History, this four-story sphere "floating" in a glass square is astonishing. Even if you're suffering from museum overload, the Rose Center will lift your spirits. The center's **Hayden Planetarium** features spectacular space shows (every half-hour Mon–Fri 10:30am–4:30pm, Wed from 11am; Sat 10:30am–5pm). *See p 55.*

11 **The Dakota and Strawberry Fields.** The 1884 apartment house with dark trim and dramatic gables, dormers, and oriel windows is best known as the spot where its most famous resident, John Lennon, was gunned down on December 8, 1980 (Yoko Ono still lives here). Directly across the street from the Dakota in Central Park is the Strawberry Fields memorial to the songwriter and peace activist. A must for serious Beatles fans. *1 W. 72nd St. (at Central Park West) & Central Park btw. 71st & 74th sts.*

12 **Telepan.** Just a short stroll from Lincoln Center or Central Park, Telepan offers farm-fresh seasonal dishes prepared by acclaimed chef Bill Telepan. Visit in the spring and Chef Telepan might sprinkle fiddleheads, fresh ramps, and spring peas into his innovative creations, such as pea pancakes with wild mushrooms (a fan favorite), pea agnolotti, and spring vegetables. *72 W. 69th St. (btw. Columbus & Central Park West).* ☎ *212/580-4300. www.telepan-ny.com. $$$.*

13 ★★ **Lincoln Center for the Performing Arts.** New York has countless performing arts venues, but none so multifaceted as Lincoln Center—presenting world-class opera, ballet, dramatic theater, jazz, symphonies, and more. After a long day on your feet, relax on the outdoor plaza in front of the fountains or on the tilting roof lawn. At Christmastime, the light displays are lovely, and on summer evenings, the plaza becomes an outdoor dance party. *See p 143.*

The Best **in Three Days**

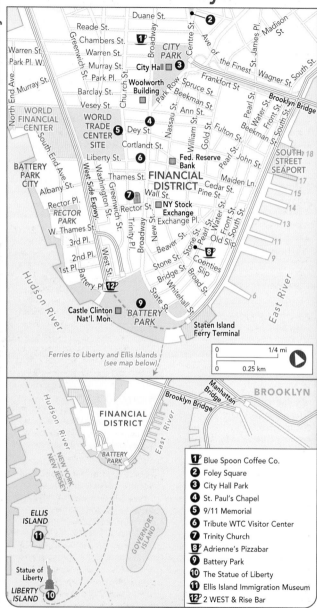

1. Blue Spoon Coffee Co.
2. Foley Square
3. City Hall Park
4. St. Paul's Chapel
5. 9/11 Memorial
6. Tribute WTC Visitor Center
7. Trinity Church
8. Adrienne's Pizzabar
9. Battery Park
10. The Statue of Liberty
11. Ellis Island Immigration Museum
12. 2 WEST & Rise Bar

Explore the city's beginnings, its turbulent recent history, and its dynamic present in Lower Manhattan. You'll find old Dutch influences and cobblestoned streets, a center of city government and world finance, the beautiful waterfront Battery Park looking over the Statue of Liberty and Ellis Island, and a neighborhood that still bears the scars of the September 11, 2001, terrorist attacks. (Don't miss the memorial at the World Trade Center site.) *Note: In 2012 Hurricane Sandy took its toll on Lower Manhattan. As a result, at press time Ellis Island remains closed until further notice.* We also recommend you start this tour early and book visits to both the memorial and Lady Liberty in advance. For more details on southern Manhattan, see p 60. START: **Subway 4, 5, or 6 to Brooklyn Bridge/City Hall.**

1 Blue Spoon Coffee Co. Kick off your day with a pick-me-up at this favorite of City Hall workers. It serves Intelligentsia brand coffee and tea, Balthazar breads, plus bagels, panini, muffins, and more. *76 Chambers St. (btw. Broadway & Church).* ☎ *212/619-7230. http:// bluespooncoffee.com. $.*

2 ★ **Foley Square.** It's hard to believe that this dignified urban landscape was once a fetid swamp and, in the 19th century, one of the city's most notorious slums, Five Points. Today, with its ring of colonnaded courthouse buildings, Foley Square bustles with judiciary industry. It's also one of the most filmed places in the five boroughs. The exterior of the 1913 **NY State Supreme Court Building** (60 Centre St.) is where Kris Kringle goes on trial in *Miracle on 34th Street* (the original) and also looks very familiar if you were a *Law & Order* fan. The imposing 1932 **Thurgood Marshall U.S. Courthouse** (40 Centre St.) was designed by Cass Gilbert. *Bounded by Centre, Worth & Lafayette sts. Subway: 4/5/6 to Brooklyn Bridge/City Hall.*

3 City Hall Park. City Hall has been the seat of NYC government since 1812. Individual tours of the inside are available Thursdays at 10am, but if that's not an option, you can appreciate the handsome park, highlighted by flickering gaslight lamps, and the 1811 building's French Renaissance exterior. Abraham Lincoln was laid in state in the soaring rotunda. Equally grand is the colossal **Municipal Building** (1 Centre St. at Chambers St.), built on the other side of Centre Street in 1915 by McKim, Mead & White; it was the celebrated firm's first "skyscraper." Across Broadway at no. 233 is that temple of commerce known as the ★ **Woolworth Building.** Built from the proceeds of a nickel-and-dime empire in 1913, this neo-Gothic masterpiece is the work of Cass Gilbert; at press time, the public was not allowed inside the building. *City Hall Park (btw. Broadway & Park Row).*

4 ★★ **St. Paul's Chapel.** Manhattan's only surviving pre-Revolutionary church was built in 1766 to resemble London's St. Martin-in-the-Fields. With a light, elegant Georgian interior, the chapel was a refuge for rescue workers after September 11. It is at St. Paul's that the story of 9/11 is most vividly on display, with artifacts, impromptu shrines, and donations from around the world. The peaceful churchyard in back is filled with 18th- and 19th-century tombstones. ⏱ *25 min. 209 Broadway (at Fulton St.). ☎ 212/233-4164. www.trinitywall-street.org. Mon–Fri 10am–6pm, Sat 10am–4pm, Sun 7am–3pm. Subway: 2/3 to Park Place; 1/9/4/5/A to Fulton St./Broadway/Nassau.*

5 ★★★ **9/11 Memorial.** The Twin Towers dominated the city's skyline after their construction in 1973, and visitors from around the world have made pilgrimages to this site since their destruction during the September 11, 2001, terrorist attacks. A permanent memorial, *Reflecting Absence*, designed by Michael Arad and Peter Walker, converts the footprints of the Twin Towers into large reflective pools, incorporating the largest man-made waterfalls in North America. A directory of names of 9/11 victims (inscribed around the pools) is available at **www.911memorial. org** or through the site's free "Explore 9/11" iPhone app. Passes for *Reflecting Absence* and the Memorial Site can be attained at the nearby preview site and

minimuseum (20 Vesey St.; ☎ 212/267-2047). Once at the memorial, you'll be surrounded by the bustling construction of Daniel Libeskind's 1,776-foot-tall (533m) **One World Trade Center** and the site's four other new buildings. A winglike steel and glass canopy, designed by Catalan architect Santiago Calatrava, will shelter the nearby World Trade Center transportation hub. (At press time, the official National September 11 Memorial & Museum was scheduled to open in the spring of 2014.) ⏱ *2 hr. 1 Albany St. (at Greenwich St.). www.911memorial.org. Opens daily at 10am; closing time subject to change. Subway: A/C to World Trade Center; N/R to Cortland St.*

6 **Tribute WTC Visitor Center.** This center at the WTC site's south border was created by the nonprofit September 11th Families' Association. It offers daily walking tours ($22), led by people whose lives were affected by the disaster. *90 Liberty St. ☎ 212/393-9160. www.tributewtc.org. Subway: A/C to World Trade Center; N/R to Cortland St.*

The new One World Trade Center building, adjacent to the 9/11 Memorial.

Trinity Church's cemetery, where founding father Alexander Hamilton is buried.

7 ★★ **Trinity Church.** This lovely neo-Gothic marvel was consecrated in 1846 and is still active today. The main doors, modeled on the doors in Florence's Baptistry, are decorated with biblical scenes; inside are splendid stained-glass windows. Among those buried in the pretty churchyard are Alexander Hamilton and Robert Fulton. ○ *25 min. 79 Broadway (at Wall St.).* ☎ *212/602-0800. www. trinitywallstreet.org. Mon–Fri 7am–6pm, Sat 8am–4pm, Sun 7am–4pm. Subway: 4/5 to Wall St.*

8 ★ **Adrienne's Pizzabar.** The narrow historic Stone Street (p 62) is lined with cafes, taverns, and restaurants. In summer, the street is closed to traffic and tables are set out on the cobblestones. You might try Adrienne's, which serves square thin-crust pizza. *54 Stone St. (btw. William & Pearl sts.).* ☎ *212/248-3838. $–$$.*

9 ★★ **Battery Park.** Stroll the landscaped park and riverside walkway for sweeping views of New York Harbor, the Statue of Liberty, and the Verrazano Bridge. It's a breezy, scenic spot to appreciate the scope of the mighty harbor—the engine behind the city's monumental growth ever since Henry Hudson and his wooden sailing ship rode the blue swells to shore. The park's centerpiece is the damaged 22-ton bronze sphere that once stood in the World Trade Center plaza. *From State St. to New York Harbor.* ☎ *212/344-3496. www.thebattery.org. Free admission. Subway: 4/5 to Bowling Green; 1/9 to South Ferry.*

10 ★ **kids** **The Statue of Liberty.** For the millions who arrived in New York by ship, Lady Liberty was their first glimpse of America. A gift from France to the U.S., the statue was designed by sculptor Frédéric-Auguste Bartholdi and unveiled on October 28, 1886.

Note: Save yourself a potentially 3-hour wait and buy and print tickets ahead of time. Tickets sell out daily by noon. After a renovation, the pedestal and crown reopened to visitors on July 4, 2013. To visit the crown you will have to climb 354 un-air-conditioned steps. Check the website for other precautions and restrictions before buying tickets. Visitors can also explore the Statue of Liberty Museum, peer into the inner structure through a glass ceiling near the base of the statue, and enjoy views from the observation deck instead. *Tip:* The Staten Island Ferry (www.siferry.com), a free 25-minute trip—not to be confused with the official Statue Cruises, which docks at Liberty island—provides spectacular skyline views of Manhattan and is a wonderful way to see the harbor. You'll pass by (although not stop at) Lady Liberty and Ellis Island. ⏱ *1 hr. (Statue Cruise ferry: 15 min.). On Liberty Island in New York Harbor.* ☎ *212/363-3200 (general info) or 877/523-9849 (tickets). www.nps. gov/stli & www.statuecruises.com. Ferry tickets to Liberty Island including access to the crown $20 adults, $17 seniors, $12 children 4–12. Daily 9am–4pm (last ferry departs around 3pm); extended hours in summer. Subway: 4/5 to Bowling Green; 1/9 to South Ferry.*

⑫ ★★★ kids Ellis Island Immigration Museum. For 62 years (1892–1954), this was the main point of entry for newcomers to America. Today it's one of New York's most moving attractions—particularly for the 40 percent of Americans whose ancestors passed through the immigration center here. It skillfully describes coming to America through the eyes of the immigrants. At press time, the museum was not scheduled to open in 2013 due to damage inflicted by Hurricane Sandy. Check the website for updates. ⏱ *2 hr. (Statue Cruise ferry: 10 min. from Liberty Island).* ☎ *212/363-3200. www.nps.gov/elis. Daily 9:30am–5pm; extended hours in summer. Subway: 4/5 to Bowling Green; 1/9 to South Ferry.*

⑬ ★ 2West. Finish your tour with a cocktail and a bite to eat in the warm, elegant 2West restaurant/lounge inside the Ritz-Carlton Battery Park, just across the street from the Museum of Jewish Heritage (p 53). Or spring for the restaurant's popular weekend brunch (about $60 per person). *2 West St.* ☎ *212/248-3838. www.ritzcarlton. com. $$$.* ●

The Statue of Liberty.

20

Romantic New York

Previous page: A room in the Stettheimer Doll House.

New York is revered for its high-energy, never-say-die attitude. But to me, the city harbors a romantic streak as wide as the Hudson River. This tour introduces you to places that are best discovered as a twosome. START: Subway 4, 5, or 6 to 86th Street.

❶ ★★ The Metropolitan Museum of Art. The city's premier museum stays open until 9pm on weekend nights. It's a lovely time to visit—quieter, with fewer visitors. You'll have some rooms almost all to yourself (and the Met security team, of course). You can combine some leisurely gallery hopping with cocktails in the Balcony Bar overlooking the Great Hall. When the weather warms, rendezvous for drinks on the Roof Garden with spectacular views of Central Park and the skyline that surrounds it. To the west, the tip of a real Egyptian obelisk peers above the park tree line. Dating from about 1500 B.C., it was a gift from the Egyptian government in the late 19th century. Its name alone, Cleopatra's Needle, conjures up ageless romance. *See p 12.*

❷ ★★ The Lake. Ella Fitzgerald sang "I love the rowing on Central Park Lake" in "The Lady Is a Tramp," and when you see the shimmering waters edged by weeping willows and Japanese cherry trees, you'll understand why it inspired songwriters Rodgers and Hart. The green banks along the man-made lake slope gently toward the water and make for an ideal picnic spot. You can rent a rowboat for two at the neo-Victorian Loeb Boathouse at the east end of the lake. The boathouse also has a restaurant and a seasonal outside bar with seating overlooking the lake. It's a thoroughly pleasant place to enjoy a cool summer cocktail. *Midpark from 71st to 78th sts.*

❸ ★ FireBird. A jewel box of a Russian restaurant on Times Square's Restaurant Row, FireBird is an homage to the opulent decadence of czarist Russia. Head upstairs to the parlor for a cocktail and a sampling of Russian delicacies. You'll feel like royalty inside a gilded Fabergé egg. *365 W. 46th St. (btw. Eighth & Ninth aves.).* ☎ *212/586-0244. www.firebird restaurant.com. $$$–$$$$.*

❹ Sheep Meadow. Skip the horse-drawn carriage rides, which are pretty pricey (roughly $40 for 20 min.). Head to the Sheep Meadow instead, a large green swath in lower Central Park that actually was once a grazing ground for sheep. It's got stupendous views of the Central Park South skyline pillowed in trees, perfect for a picnic. *Midpark btw. 66th & 69th sts.*

The elegant entrance to FireBird.

❺ ★★ The Plaza. This historic confection has played a part in countless romances. Newlyweds Scott and Zelda Fitzgerald famously frolicked in the fountain out front. And who can forget the poignant final scene in *The Way We Were*, when Barbra Streisand and Robert Redford say good-bye in front of the Plaza? The scene was lovingly re-created on TV's *Sex and the City*. Toast to bittersweet romance in the swank Champagne Bar. *768 Fifth Ave. (at 59th St.).* ☎ *212/759-3000. www.theplazany.com. Subway: N/R/W to Fifth Ave. & 59th St.*

❻ ★★ Tiffany & Co. "A kiss may be grand, but it won't pay the rental"—as the folks at Tiffany well know. Seal the deal with a diamond ring from this classic jeweler. *727 Fifth Ave. (btw. 56th & 57th sts.).* ☎ *212/755-8000. Subway: E/M to Fifth Ave./53rd St.*

Tiffany & Co.'s iconic blue bag.

❼ Lincoln Center Plaza. On a warm summer night, grab your partner and dance with romantic abandon during "Midsummer Night Swing," the sexy dance party on Josie Robertson Plaza. Every night is a different dance theme, from salsa to swing to ballroom. The fountains and floodlights of the plaza are particularly seductive at dusk. Go to **www. lincolncenter.org** for the latest information.

❽ ★★ The Rink in Rockefeller Center. A romantic winter rendezvous on the ice-skating rink in the center's Lower Plaza is cliché, but just try to resist a swirl around the ice during the holidays, with the spectacular Rock Center Christmas tree glittering from above. Avoid crowds by going early or late. Don't skate? Have a drink in the Sea Grill—which directly faces the rink—and watch the action. *Lower Plaza, Rockefeller Center (btw. 49th & 50th sts).* ☎ *212/332-7654. Admission $20–$25 adults, $12–$15 seniors & children 11 & under; skate rental $10. Mid-Oct to mid-Apr; call for hours. See p 8.*

❾ The Whispering Gallery. Not only is the tiled Gustavino ceiling outside the Grand Central Oyster Bar a beauty, but it creates an acoustical phenomenon. Stand facing one of the pillars with your loved one facing the one directly opposite and whisper sweet nothings. You'll be able to hear one another—and no one else can listen in. *Grand Central Station, 42nd St. & Park Ave.* ☎ *212/340-2210. www.grandcentralterminal.com. Subway: 4/5/6 to 42nd St./Grand Central.*

The River Café.

10 ★ **Le Gigot.** Sometimes the best recipe for romance is a warm, intimate spot where candles flicker seductively. At this classic little Provençal bistro in the West Village, you can dine on bouillabaisse or a hearty cassoulet. Look around; you're not the only ones on a romantic rendezvous. *18 Cornelia St. (btw. Bleecker & West 4th sts.).* ☎ *212/627-3737. www.legigot restaurant.com. $$$.*

11 ★★ **Harbor Cruise.** Whether you're on a simple spin around the island or an elegant dinner cruise, seeing Manhattan from the water is a thrill. That old reliable, **Circle Line** (www.circleline42.com), has the most options, from 2-hour harbor cruises to summer live-music cruises, from $29 to $39. Circle Line leaves from Pier 83 (W. 42nd St.). **Bateaux New York** (www. bateauxnewyork.com) runs dinner cruises in sleek glass boats to the accompaniment of live jazz, from $55 to $140. It leaves from Pier 61 at Chelsea Piers (W. 23rd St.).

12 ★ **The River Café.** The River Café sits on the Brooklyn waterfront practically underneath the Brooklyn Bridge, with magnificent views of downtown Manhattan. Even if you don't come for dinner, you can sit on the terrace, sip a cocktail, and drink in the views. *1 Water St., Brooklyn.* ☎ *718/522-5200. www. rivercafe.com. $$$–$$$$.*

New York Money

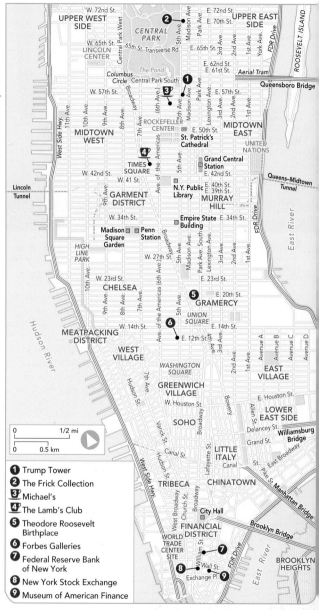

1 Trump Tower
2 The Frick Collection
3 Michael's
4 The Lamb's Club
5 Theodore Roosevelt Birthplace
6 Forbes Galleries
7 Federal Reserve Bank of New York
8 New York Stock Exchange
9 Museum of American Finance

The city has long been a mecca for ambitious types. The robber barons of the 19th century, such men as Henry Clay Frick and J. P. Morgan, thrived here. So have their modern-day counterparts, including moguls Donald Trump and Mike Bloomberg. These are the landmarks that define them all. START: **Subway F to 57th Street.**

1 Trump Tower. This bold and brassy place is definitely not your average shopping mall. The gold signage on the 1983 building practically screams, "Look at me!" Step inside to view the six-story mirrored atrium and the waterfall cascading down a pink-granite wall. Admire the glitzy displays of such luxury shops as Cartier and Asprey of London as you glide up the escalators. *725 Fifth Ave. (btw. 56th & 57th sts.).* ☎ *212/832-2000. Subway: B/D/F/M to 57th St.*

2 ★★★ The Frick Collection. Industrialist Henry Clay Frick, who controlled the steel industry in Pittsburgh in the late 19th century, began collecting art after he made his first million. Architects Carrère & Hastings built this palatial French neoclassical mansion in 1914 to house both Frick's family and his art (Frick chose to live in Manhattan

Trump Tower on Fifth Avenue.

instead of his native Pennsylvania, legend has it, to avoid the soot from the steel mills). This living testament to New York's Gilded Age is graced with paintings from Frick's collection: works by Titian, Gainsborough, Rembrandt, Turner, Vermeer, El Greco, and Goya. A highlight is the Fragonard Room, which contains the sensual rococo series *The Progress of Love.* The house is particularly stunning in its Christmas finery. ⏱ *2 hr. 1 E. 70th St. (at Fifth Ave.).* ☎ *212/288-0700. www.frick.org. Admission $18 adults, $15 seniors, $10 students. Children under 10 not admitted; children under 16 must be accompanied by an adult. Tues–Sat 10am–6pm, Sun 11am–5pm. Closed Mon & all major holidays. Subway: 6 to 68th St. Bus: M1/2/3/4.*

3 ★ Michael's. The New York media and other members of the elite lunch at Michael's, a spacious spot in a landmark building—and we're talking everybody from Barbara Walters to Bill Clinton. You know your place in the pecking order when you are seated in this power palace—even though the fresh flowers, pretty paintings, and sunny California cuisine work to soften the blow. *24 W. 55th St. (btw. Fifth & Sixth aves.).* ☎ *212/767-0555. $$$–$$$$.* Of course, if you're a media mogul in training, you may be too pressed for time to glad-hand at Michael's. Grab lunch to go instead from a food cart, such as Daisy May's BBQ, which dishes out some of New York's best barbecue. *52nd St. & Park Ave. www.daisy maysbbq.com. $.*

The Frick Collection.

4️⃣ The Lambs Club. This new/old power gathering spot, formerly a 1920s hangout of New York literati, thespians, and theater movers and shakers, was brought back to life by chef Geoffrey Zakarian in 2010. In its new incarnation, the club now attracts . . . literati, thespians, and theater movers and shakers as well as titans of fashion and finance who, surrounded by dark oak walls and lush red leather banquettes, convene here at breakfast, lunch, and dinner to deal and dream. *132 W. 44th St. (btw. Sixth Ave. & Broadway).* ☎ *212/997-5262. www. thelambsclub.com. $$–$$$.*

5️⃣ ★ Theodore Roosevelt Birthplace. America's 26th president was born and raised here (the original house was destroyed in 1916 and then faithfully reconstructed in 1923). It was decorated by Roosevelt's wife and sisters with many original furnishings. The restored house contains five period rooms, two museum galleries, and a bookstore. Roosevelt was the nemesis of the robber barons. Known as the Trust Buster, he broke up monopolies in such industries as railroads and steel to protect the public interest. ⏱ *45 min. 28 E. 20th St. (btw. Broadway & Park Ave. South).* ☎ *212/260-1616. www. nps.gov/thrb. Free admission. Tues– Sat 9am–5pm. Subway: 6 to 23rd St.*

6️⃣ ★ 🅺🅸🅳🆂 Forbes Galleries. Publishing magnate Malcolm Forbes was a passionate collector. Toy soldiers (10,000 or so), early-edition Monopoly boards, and toy boats (more than 500) are the highlights here. (The real stars of the Forbes collection, 12 Fabergé Imperial Eggs, were sold, fittingly, to a Russian tycoon in 2004.) Changing exhibits have included a selection of letters written by first ladies, jeweled flowers and fruit by Cartier, and historically accurate miniature rooms. You can book a free tour in advance. ⏱ *45 min. 62 Fifth Ave. (at 12th St.).* ☎ *212/206-5548. www.forbesgalleries.com. Free admission; children under 16 must be*

The Federal Reserve building, which holds $90 billion in gold in its vaults.

The New York Stock Exchange.

accompanied by an adult. *Tues–Wed & Fri–Sat 10am–4pm. Subway: 4/5/6 to 14th St.*

❼ Federal Reserve Bank of New York. This is where they keep the gold—$90 billion of it. It rests 50 feet (15m) below sea level. You can tour the gold vaults and the bank's museum on a free 45-minute tour, but be sure to book at least 1 week in advance. *① 1 hr. 33 Liberty St. (btw. William & Nassau sts.). ☎ 212/720-6130. frbnytours@ ny.frb.org. www.newyorkfed.org. Subway: 4/5 to Wall St.*

❽ New York Stock Exchange. The serious action is here on Wall Street, a narrow lane dating from the 17th century. At its heart is the NYSE, the world's largest securities exchange. The NYSE came into being in 1792, when merchants met daily under a nearby buttonwood tree to trade U.S. bonds that had funded the Revolutionary War. In 1903, traders moved into this Beaux Arts building designed by George Post. The NYSE is still surrounded by heavy security and is not open to the public. *18 Broad St. (btw. Wall St. & Exchange Place). ☎ 212/656-3000. www.nyse.com.*

❾ ★ Museum of American Finance. This museum explores

the country's free-market traditions and spirit of entrepreneurship. It is housed in a landmark Benjamin Morris–designed building from the late 1920s, with major exhibitions filling the building's grand mezzanine. *① 45 min. 48 Wall St. (at William St.). ☎ 212/908-4100. www. moaf.org. Admission $8 adults, $5 seniors & students, free for kids 6 and under; free admission on Sat. Tues–Sat 10am–4pm. Subway: 4/5/2/3 to Wall St.*

The Charging Bull, symbol of Wall Street, in Bowling Green Park.

New York **with Kids**

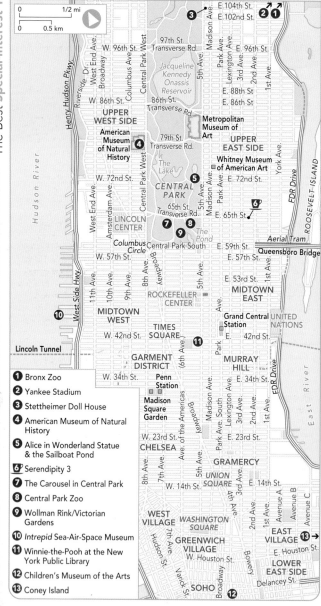

1 Bronx Zoo
2 Yankee Stadium
3 Stettheimer Doll House
4 American Museum of Natural History
5 Alice in Wonderland Statue & the Sailboat Pond
6 Serendipity 3
7 The Carousel in Central Park
8 Central Park Zoo
9 Wollman Rink/Victorian Gardens
10 *Intrepid* Sea-Air-Space Museum
11 Winnie-the-Pooh at the New York Public Library
12 Children's Museum of the Arts
13 Coney Island

Beneath its noise, grit, and air of jaded cynicism, New York City is extremely kid-friendly. It opens its arms to kids of all ages, with some of the top children's attractions in the country, magical kid-centric holidays, and a world of treats for the eyes, ears, and tummy. What kid can resist? Just be sure to budget 3 to 4 days if you want to fit in everything on this tour. START: Subway 2 or 5 to East Tremont Avenue/West Farms Square.

❶ ★★★ kids Bronx Zoo. The largest urban wildlife conservation facility in America, the Bronx Zoo has some 4,000 animals roaming 265 acres (106 hectares). It's hard to believe that you're actually in the Bronx as you watch lions, zebras, and gazelles roam the African Plains, a re-created savanna. Don't miss Tiger Mountain, featuring Siberian tigers, or the Congo Gorilla Forest, where 23 lowland gorillas, assorted monkeys, and other species live in a 6½-acre (2.6-ha) African rainforest environment. ⏱ 4–5 hr. Fordham Rd. & Bronx River Pkwy. ☎ 718/652-8400. www.bronxzoo.com. Mon–Fri 10am–4:30pm, Sat–Sun 10am–5:30pm (extended summer & holiday hours). Admission $17 adults, $15 seniors, $13 children 3–12, free for kids 2 & under. Check website for online discounts. Subway: 2/5 to E. Tremont Ave./W. Farms Sq.

❷ ★★★ kids Yankee Stadium. Is there a better way to spend a sun-dappled afternoon or warm summer evening than at a baseball game at Yankee Stadium? And the quickest and most convenient way to get to the stadium is the subway. ⏱ 4 hr. 1 E. 161st St. (Jerome Ave.), the Bronx. ☎ 718/293-6000. www.yankees.com. Tickets $15–$65. Subway: B/D/4 to 161st St.

❸ ★★★ kids Stettheimer Doll House. This remarkable dollhouse in the Museum of the City of New York was the creation of Carrie Walter Stettheimer, a theater set designer who, with her two equally talented sisters, entertained the city's avant-garde artist community in the 1920s. Among the exquisite furnishings are period wallpaper, paper lampshades, and an art gallery featuring miniatures of such famous works as Marcel Duchamp's *Nude Descending a Staircase*. The museum has more vintage dollhouses and timeless toys on display. ⏱ 1½ hr. Museum of the City of New York, 1220 Fifth Ave. (103rd St.). ☎ 212/534-1672. www.mcny.org. Tues–Sun 10am–5pm. Admission $10 adults, $6 students & seniors, free for children 12 & under, $20 families (2 adults plus kids). Subway: 6 to 103rd St.

❹ ★★★ kids American Museum of Natural History. One word: ★ dinosaurs, which devour the entrance hall and take up the entire fourth floor. Not to mention diamonds as big as the Ritz, and much more. See p 54.

❺ ★★ kids Central Park's Alice in Wonderland Statue & Sailboat Pond. The 1959 bronze statue of Alice sitting on a giant mushroom is catnip to the little ones. The Sailboat Pond, officially called Conservatory Water, is an ornamental pond where kids can sail miniature boats or watch radio-powered model yachts compete in racing regattas. *Central Park, east side from 72nd to 75th sts.*

6 **kids** **Serendipity 3.** The ice-cream sundaes are legendary at this whimsical Upper East Side dessert palace, which also serves kid-friendly burgers, pastas, and chicken potpie. Try the "Shake, Batter & Bowl": half a chicken, fried and oven-roasted, and French fries. *225 E. 60th St. (btw. Second & Third aves.).* ☎ *212/838-3531. www.serendipity3.com. $$.*

7 ★★ **kids** **The Carousel in Central Park**. A quarter of a million children ride these vintage hand-carved horses every year. *See p 3.*

8 ★★ **kids** **Central Park Zoo.** The zoo dates from the mid–19th century, when caged animals on loan from circuses were put on display near the Arsenal. The current zoo was built in 1988 to replace a 1934 WPA-built structure. Today the zoo's 5½ acres (2.2 ha) house more than 400 animals, among them sea lions, polar bears, and penguins. In the small **Tisch Children's Zoo,** kids can feed and pet tame farm animals. Check out the **Delacorte Clock,** with six dancing animals designed by the Italian sculptor Andrea Spadini. *See p 107.*

Skaters on Wollman Rink.

9 ★★ **kids** **Trump (Wollman) Rink/Victorian Gardens.** The small ice-skating rink at Rockefeller Center is right in the center of Midtown action, but this much bigger cold-weather rink in Central Park is built for stretching out and perfecting your moves. Plus, it has views of skyscrapers along Central Park South. In the summer, it's transformed into the **Victorian Gardens Amusement Park,** which has old-fashioned carnival rides for young children. *See p 107.*

10 ★★ **kids** *Intrepid Sea-Air-Space Museum.* The aircraft carrier known as the "Fighting I" served the U.S. Navy for 31 years, suffering bomb attacks, kamikaze strikes, and a torpedo shot. It's now a very cool sea, air, and space museum on the New York waterfront. You can crawl inside a wooden sub from the American Revolution, inspect a missile submarine, and manipulate the controls in the cockpit of an A-6 Intruder. ***Note:*** Summers are crowded; get here early or buy tickets online. ⏱ *1½ hr. Pier 86, 12th Ave. & 46th St.* ☎ *212/245-0072. http://intrepidmuseum.org. Admission $24 adults, $20 students & seniors, $19 children 3–17, free for children 2 & under. Apr–Sept Mon–Fri 10am–5pm, Sat–Sun 10am–6pm; Oct–Mar Tues–Sun 10am–5pm. Bus: M42 to 12th St. & Hudson Ave. Subway: 1/2/3/7/9/A/C/E/S to 42nd St./Times Sq.*

11 ★★ **kids** **New York Public Library.** The original Winnie-the-Pooh bear, the little stuffed animal owned and cherished by Christopher Robin Milne, is on display in the main branch's Children's Center, along with Eeyore, Piglet, Kanga, and Tigger. From October to March **Bryant Park,** behind the library, has ice-skating in addition to its year-round carousel. *See p 8.*

Fighter planes on the deck of the Intrepid.

⑫ ★★ kids Children's Museum of the Arts. More creative play space than stodgy museum, this art-themed duplex has a paint-splashed charm. It's a great place for budding artists to express themselves. ⏱ *2 hr. 182 Lafayette St. (btw. Broome & Grand sts.). ☎ 212/274-0986. www.cmany. org. Admission $11, free for children under 1. Mon & Wed–Sun noon–5pm (Thurs–Fri to 6pm). Subway: 6 to Spring St. or N/R to Prince St.*

⑬ ★ kids Coney Island. This classic summer playground has carny rides, wooden boardwalks, and breezy salt air. It's a long subway ride out, but once you're here you can ride the 1927 **Cyclone** roller coaster or the 1920 **Wonder Wheel;** play at **Luna Park,** the first new amusement park built on Coney Island in 40 years; or just splash in the sea. *1208 Surf Ave., Brooklyn. ☎ 718/372-5159. www. coneyisland.com; www.lunaparknyc. com. Memorial Day to Labor Day daily noon to late evening; Easter to Memorial Day and Labor Day to end of Oct weekends only noon to late evening. Cyclone ticket $8, Wonder Wheel ticket $6, unlimited-ride wristbands $29. Subway: D/N to Coney Island/Stillwell Ave.; F/Q to W. 8th St.*

Holiday Magic

New York celebrates the holidays with glitter and gusto. On Thanksgiving, the **Macy's Day Parade** rolls through town; find yourself a perch along the parade route or, if you're smart, a hotel room with a view of the festivities. Join the locals the night before for what's become a street party around the Museum of Natural History to watch the inflating of the giant parade balloons. At Christmastime, head for the ever-popular holiday revue at Radio City Music Hall, the **Christmas Spectacular** (☎ 212/307-1000; www.radiocity.com; tickets $45–$250). In the Bronx, the New York Botanical Gardens is the site for the wonderful **Holiday Train Show,** where vintage model trains zip around miniature reproductions of well-known New York landmarks—all made *entirely out of plant materials* (☎ 718/817-8700; www.nybg.org; $20 adults, $7 children 2–12, free for children 1 & under). Take the 20-minute Metro-North Railroad from Grand Central to the Botanical Gardens stop. Both the Radio City show and the train show run from November through early January.

Literary Gotham

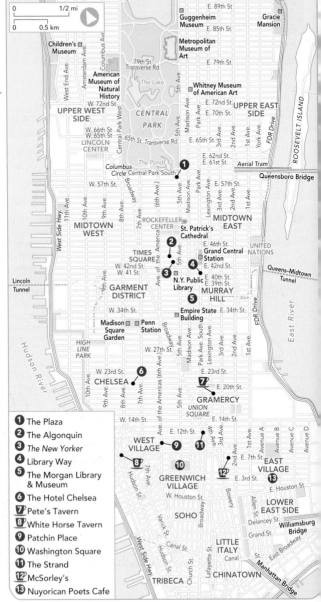

0   1/2 mi
0   0.5 km

- **1** The Plaza
- **2** The Algonquin
- **3** *The New Yorker*
- **4** Library Way
- **5** The Morgan Library & Museum
- **6** The Hotel Chelsea
- **7** Pete's Tavern
- **8** White Horse Tavern
- **9** Patchin Place
- **10** Washington Square
- **11** The Strand
- **12** McSorley's
- **13** Nuyorican Poets Cafe

There is something about the compelling fabric of New York life that has long inspired writers. The home of the publishing industry, New York is a town that embraces the written word. Readings by big-name as well as undiscovered authors are a daily occurrence at venues throughout the city. What follows is a tour of some of the city's past and present literary landmarks. START: **Subway N, R, or W to Fifth Avenue and 59th Street.**

❶ ★★ The Plaza. Eloise lived here, of course; the celebrated children's book heroine won the hotel "Literary Landmark" status in 1998. *Eloise* was written in 1955 by performer Kay Thompson during her stay at the Plaza, and the famous portrait of the mischievous little girl is still displayed in the renovated lobby. *See p 9.*

❷ ★ The Algonquin. In the 1920s, this hotel was where such notable literati as James Thurber and the acid-tongued Dorothy Parker met to drink and trade bons mots at the so-called Round Table. The table still has a place of honor in the Rose Room, but be warned: It's rectangular. The richly appointed lobby is also atmospheric. *59 W. 44th St. (btw. Fifth & Sixth aves.).* ☎ *212/840-6800. www.algonquinhotel.com. Subway: B/D/F/M to 42nd St.*

❸ The former *New Yorker* offices. America's most celebrated literary magazine came into being at the Algonquin Round Table, just a block away from its former office space here. Over the decades, it has featured such writers as E. B. White, John Cheever, John Updike, and Calvin Trillin, and you'll find their names and others on a plaque. (Today, *The New Yorker* offices are in the Condé Nast building at 4 Times Sq.) *25 W. 43rd St. (btw. Fifth & Sixth aves.). Subway: B/D/F/M to 42nd St.*

❹ ★ Library Way. Along 41st Street between Park and Fifth, you'll see bronze plaques embedded in the sidewalk. There are 96 in total, and all feature quotations from literature or poetry. Walking west along this street leads you to the legendary New York Public Library. *41st St. (btw. Park & Fifth aves.). Subway: B/D/F/M to 42nd St.*

❺ ★★ The Morgan Library & Museum. The former private library of financier John Pierpont Morgan contains one of the most important collections of rare books and manuscripts in the world. It was not Morgan himself who bartered with booksellers but his personal librarian, Belle da Costa Greene, a light-skinned African American who passed herself off as white to gain

The Living Word sculpture by Xu Bing in the Morgan Library.

The Hotel Chelsea.

entree into Morgan's world. Morgan gave her carte blanche (money was no object) to buy some of the world's rarest manuscripts, a job she ably carried out for more than 40 years. ○ *2 hr. 29 E. 36th St. (btw. Park & Madison aves.).* ☎ *212/685-0610. www.themorgan. org. Admission $15 adults, $10 seniors, students & children 13–15, free children for 12 & under. Tues–Thurs 10:30am–5pm, Fri 10:30am–9pm, Sat 10am–6pm, Sun 11am–6pm. Subway: B/D/F/N/Q/R/M to 34th St.*

6 The Hotel Chelsea. Built in 1884, the Chelsea became a hotel in 1905 where artists and writers were encouraged to stay indefinitely. Among the writers who did: Mark Twain, Thomas Wolfe, Dylan Thomas, O. Henry, Arthur Miller, and Sam Shepard (with his then-lover Patti Smith). The hotel is closed, used primarily now for film and television production, but you can still admire its grandeur from outside. *222 W. 23rd St. (btw. Seventh & Eighth aves.).* ☎ *212/243-3700. www.hotelchelsea.com. Subway: 1/9/A/C to 23rd St.*

7 Pete's Tavern. The literary ghosts abound within ancient Pete's Tavern. A New York City landmark that claims to be the oldest continuing dining establishment in New York (1864), it was in the second booth from the front where, in 1906, writer O. Henry was said to have penned his Christmas fable Gift of the Magi. In 1939, writer Ludwig Bemelmans used Pete's Tavern as his office to write the first in his Madeline children's book series. These days, instead of thirsty cash-strapped writers, you are more likely to see film crews in and around Pete's trying to re-create that old literary New York look. *129 E. 18th Street (at Irving Plaza).* ☎ *212/473-7676. www.petestavern. com. $$.*

8 White Horse Tavern. This 1880 wood-frame bar was where such writers as Jack Kerouac, James Baldwin, Norman Mailer, and the Welsh poet Dylan Thomas threw down a few. Thomas, in fact, more or less drank himself to death here in November 1953 at the tender age of 39. Order a newfangled burger, wash it down with an icy ale, and toast the celebrated ghosts around you. Cash only. *567 Hudson St. (at 11th St.).* ☎ *212/243-9260. $–$$.*

9 Patchin Place. This sweet little cobblestone mews tucked off Sixth Avenue was at one time a serious literary enclave: The poet e e cummings lived at no. 4 from 1923 to 1962, the reclusive writer Djuna Barnes lived at no. 5 for 40 years, and journalist John Reed and his paramour Louise Bryant lived here while he wrote *Ten Days That Shook the World.* (The lefty magazine he wrote for, *The Masses,* was located a couple of blocks away at

Browsing the Strand.

91 Greenwich Ave.) *Patchin Place (off 10th St. & Sixth Ave.). Subway: A/B/C/D/E/F/M to W. 4th St.*

🔟 **Washington Square.** The literary history of New York is filled with references to this fabled downtown neighborhood—and why not? It's where many great writers grew up or chose to live. Novelist Henry James was born at 21 Washington Place in 1843 and later described the neighborhood in his memorable 1880 book *Washington Square* (later made into the heralded play and movie *The Heiress*). Edith Wharton, whose novels evoked the genteel days when the aristocracy ruled New York society from Washington Square, stayed briefly with her mother at 7 Washington Sq. N. Willa Cather lived at both 60 Washington Sq. S. and 82 Washington Place. *See p 77.*

⓫ ★ **The Strand.** You can spend hours browsing the "18 miles" of new and used books crammed into the high, narrow shelves of this 1927 institution/bookstore. *See p 95.*

⓬ **McSorley's.** This working 1854 saloon was immortalized by New Yorker writer Joseph Mitchell in "McSorley's Wonderful Saloon," found in his classic collection of true New York tales, Up in the Old Hotel and Other Stories. *15 E.*

7th St. (btw. Second & Third aves.). ☎ *212/474-9148. www. mcsorleysnewyork.com. $.*

⓭ **Nuyorican Poets Cafe.** What started out more than 30 years ago as the "living room salon" of East Village writer and poet Miguel Algarín has become a celebrated arts enterprise and a forum for up-and-coming poets, writers, playwrights, musicians, and comedians. Weekly poetry slams are held Friday nights. *236 E. 3rd St. (btw. aves. B & C).* ☎ *212/505-8183. www. nuyorican.org. Subway: A/B/C/D/E/ F/M to W. 4th St.*

McSorley's, an East Village institution.

New York's Architecture

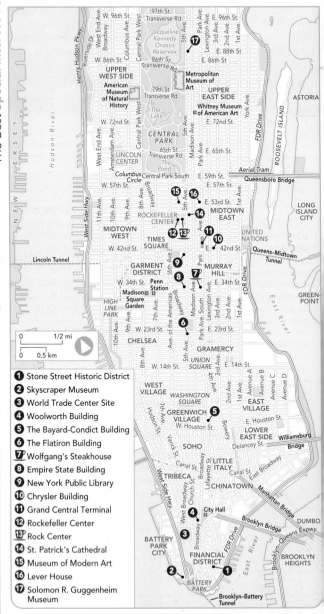

1. Stone Street Historic District
2. Skyscraper Museum
3. World Trade Center Site
4. Woolworth Building
5. The Bayard-Condict Building
6. The Flatiron Building
7. Wolfgang's Steakhouse
8. Empire State Building
9. New York Public Library
10. Chrysler Building
11. Grand Central Terminal
12. Rockefeller Center
13. Rock Center
14. St. Patrick's Cathedral
15. Museum of Modern Art
16. Lever House
17. Solomon R. Guggenheim Museum

anhattan's muscular skyline is many things: a wonderfully eclectic architectural landscape; a visual metaphor for the dynamism of America's largest city, perpetually in flux; and a stunning, three-dimensional historical record of how the Big Apple has grown—and grown up—over the years. This tour takes in a bit of all that, in 2 days. START: **Subway 4, 5, or 6 to Brooklyn Bridge/City Hall.**

❶ ★★★ Brooklyn Bridge. It took 16 very difficult years to build, but in 1883 this architectural and engineering marvel was finally finished. The 20- to 40-minute stroll on the bridge's wood-planked walkway is one of New York's must-do activities. Not only is the bridge a wonder to behold, but the views of Manhattan from it are equally stunning. *Subway: 4/5/6 to Brooklyn Bridge–City Hall.*

❷ ★ Stone Street Historic District. This narrow curve of a street, first staked out by the Dutch West India Company in the 1640s, is a find. The 15 existing brick structures lying in the shadow of Wall Street's canyons were built soon after the Great Fire of 1835 leveled the heavily commercial neighborhood. The Dutch-style facades

The Brooklyn Bridge.

trace the winding cobblestone street, now home to cafes and taverns; in the summer, the street is closed off to vehicular traffic, and the restaurants serve alfresco. *Bounded by Pearl St., Hanover Sq., S. William St. & Coenties Alley. Subway: 2/3 to Wall St.*

❸ ★ Skyscraper Museum. Wowed by New York's sheer verticality? Learn more about the technology, culture, and muscle behind it all at this small museum. Housed in the same building as the Ritz-Carlton Battery Park, it contains two galleries: one dedicated to the evolution of Manhattan's skyline, and the other to changing shows. ⏲ 1 hr. 2 West St. (museum entrance faces Battery Place). ☎ 212/968-1961. www.skyscraper.org. Admission $5 adults, $2.50 seniors & students, free for children 11 & under. Wed–Sun noon–6pm. Subway: 1 to Rector St; 4/5 to Bowling Green.*

❹ ★ One World Trade Center and the 9/11 Memorial. The enormity of the tragedy that occurred on September 11, 2001, is driven home by the sight of the massive Michael Arad–designed pools occupying the footprints of the Twin Towers. Newly risen on an adjacent site is architect Daniel Libeskind's gleaming One World Trade Center, the tallest building in the Western Hemisphere. See p 16.

❺ ★ 101 Spring Street. This five-story cast-iron building, built by architect Nicholas Whyte in 1870, remains the only intact single-use cast-iron building in SoHo. In 1968,

The Flatiron Building.

❼ ★ The Flatiron Building.

This triangular masterpiece was one of the city's most distinctive silhouettes. Its pie-slice form was the solution to a problem—filling the wedge of land created by the intersection of Fifth Avenue and Broadway. Built in 1902 and fronted with limestone and terra cotta (not iron), the Flatiron measures only 6 feet (1.8m) across at its narrow end. So called for its resemblance to the laundry appliance, it was originally named the Fuller Building, then later "Burnham's Folly" because people were certain that architect Daniel Burnham's 21-story structure would fall down. The building mainly houses publishing offices, but it has a few shops on the ground floor. The surrounding neighborhood has taken its name—the Flatiron District, home to smart restaurants and shops. *175 Fifth Ave. (at 23rd St.). Subway: R to 23rd St.*

❽ Wolfgang's Steakhouse.

Come here for a meal as bold as the architecture you're viewing—or at least stop for a drink. In a stunning historic space on the first floor of the old Vanderbilt Hotel, a 40-year veteran of Peter Luger's storied Brooklyn steakhouse opened his own meat palace in 2004. Architect Raphael Guastavino tiled the vaulted ceilings around 1910. *4 Park Ave. (at 33rd St.).* ☎ *212/889-3369. $$$$.*

minimalist Donald Judd (1928–1994) bought the former sewing factory and transformed it into a home and studio, now open to the public; the works on view in the building were set in place by the artist himself. Guided visits are $25 and offered Tuesdays, Thursdays, and Fridays. Check www.juddfoundation.org for times. *101 Spring St. (btw. Prince & Mercer sts.). Subway: N/R to Prince St.*

❻ ★ The Bayard-Condict Building.

Renowned Chicago architect Louis Sullivan was Frank Lloyd Wright's boss and, some say, his mentor. The only building Sullivan designed in New York is hidden down a nondescript NoHo street. It's a beaut, nonetheless: Constructed in 1899, the 13-story building is a creamy confection, with fanciful terra-cotta decoration and ornamental friezes. *65 Bleecker St. (btw. Broadway & Lafayette St.). Subway: 6 to Bleecker St.*

❾ ★★★ Chrysler Building.

This 1930 Art Deco masterpiece was designed to be the world's tallest building—and it was, if only for a year. In the race against other New York architects to build the tallest skyscraper of the era, William Van Alen secretly added a stainless-steel spire inside the fire shaft, hoisting it into place only after his competitors thought his building

A detail of Taurus and Orion, on the Sky Ceiling at Grand Central.

was completed. *405 Lexington Ave. (at 42nd St.). Subway: 4/5/6 to Grand Central.*

⑩ ★★★ Grand Central Terminal. This magnificent public space is also an engineering wonder. The "elevated circumferential

The Chrysler Building.

plaza," as it was called in 1913, splits Park Avenue, which is diverted around the building. The network of trains—subway and commuter—that passes through here is vast, but even more impressive is the "bridge" over the tracks, designed to support a cluster of skyscrapers. The main concourse was restored to its original glory in 1998; the *Sky Ceiling* inside depicts the constellations of the winter sky above New York. They're lit with 59 stars surrounded by dazzling 24-karat gold. Emitting light fed through fiber-optic cables, the stars in their intensities roughly replicate the magnitude of the actual stars as seen from Earth. Look carefully and you'll see a patch near one corner left unrestored—a reminder of the neglect this splendid masterpiece once endured. *42nd St. & Park Ave.* ☎ *212/340-2210. www.grand centralterminal.com. Subway: 4/5/6/7/S to 42nd St.*

⑪ ★★★ Rockefeller Center. Rock Center was erected mainly in the 1930s, when the city was mired in the Depression and in thrall to

Modern Masterpieces

If you are a fan of contemporary architecture, New York has more than its share. Check out Sir Norman Foster's addition to the Hearst Building (now **Hearst Tower**) at 300 W. 57th St. and Eighth Avenue, Kazuyo Sejima and Ryue Nishizawa/SANAA's **New Museum of Contemporary Art** at 235 Bowery (p 52), Cooper Union college's **41 Cooper Square,** designed by Morphosis architects, or the Frank Gehry–designed **IAC Building** at 555 W. 18th St. for a few examples of the changing New York landscape.

Art Deco—the latter expressed both in the building's architecture and in the art commissioned to decorate it. The focal point is the 1933 **GE Building** at 30 Rockefeller Plaza, one of the city's most impressive structures. The entrance sculpture, *Wisdom*, by Lee Lawrie, is an Art Deco masterpiece, as is the artist's *Atlas*, at the entrance court of the International Building. The sunken plaza in front of 30 Rock is overseen by the gilded statue *Prometheus* by Paul Manship. *See p 8.*

12 **Rock Center.** You won't go hungry in Rockefeller Center. In the dining and shopping concourse ($) downstairs at 30 Rock, you can pick up light meals of soup, salads, and sandwiches. If you prefer a nice sit-down lunch (and don't mind spending more), the pleasant dining rooms in the Rock Center Café (20 W. 50th St., btw. Fifth & Sixth aves.; ☎ 212/332-7620; $$) and the Sea Grill (19 W. 49th St., btw. Fifth & Sixth aves.; ☎ 212/332-7620; $$) both face the famed skating rink.

13 ★ **Lever House.** Built in 1952, this High Modern hymn to glass has undergone a spiffy renovation to restore its original sparkle. The clean-lined, relatively small skyscraper was the first in New York to employ the "curtain wall" design philosophy, with a brilliant blue-green glass facade. The bottom level is a public space. *400 Park Ave. (btw. 53rd & 54th sts.). Subway: 6 to Lexington Ave.*

14 ★★★ **Solomon R. Guggenheim Museum.** Frank Lloyd Wright's only New York edifice—built in 1959—is a brilliant feat of architecture. The Babylonian-style "inverted ziggurat" has been compared to a wedding cake or a nautilus shell, but it is full of life and movement. Just forget your fantasies about roller-skating down the ramp of the rotunda. ⏱ *1 hr. 1071 Fifth Ave. (at 89th St.).* ☎ *212/423-3500. www.guggenheim.org. Admission $22 adults, $18 seniors & students, free for children 12 & under. Sun–Wed & Fri 10am–5:45pm, Sat 10am–7:45pm. Subway: 4/5/6 to 86th St. Bus: M1/2/3/4.*

15 ★ **Riverside Church.** This majestic 2-block-long Gothic church, opened in 1930, has a long history of activism and has hosted such speakers as Martin Luther King, Jr.; Nelson Mandela; and Kofi Annan. The church's soaring bell tower is the tallest in the U.S. and an upper Manhattan landmark. Free tours of the church's breathtaking interiors—featuring artworks by Heinrich Hofmann—are given after Sunday services. ○ 1 hr. 490 Riverside Dr. (btw. 120th & 121st sts). www.theriversidechurchny.org. Subway: 1 to 116th St.

⑯ ★ Grant's Tomb. This colossal mausoleum is the crown jewel of a gorgeous stretch of Riverside Park. Ulysses S. Grant, the 18th president and the commander of the Union Army, spent the last 4 years of his life in New York; he's entombed here with his wife, Julia. The deep-red twin granite sarcophagi, viewed from a circular marble mezzanine above, are a moving, almost eerie tribute to the Civil War hero. On the monument's other side is the peaceful Sakura Park, an underrated green space with a delightful Japanese feel. ○ 20 min.

Frank Lloyd Wright's Guggenheim Museum.

Riverside Dr. & 122nd St. www.grantstomb.org. Free admission. Summer daily 9am–5pm; spring, fall & winter Thurs–Mon 9am–5pm. Subway: 1 to 125th St.

Riverside Church's bell tower is the tallest in the U.S.

NYC Free & Dirt-Cheap

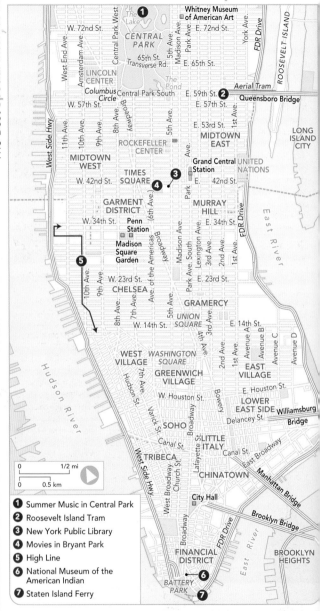

1. Summer Music in Central Park
2. Roosevelt Island Tram
3. New York Public Library
4. Movies in Bryant Park
5. High Line
6. National Museum of the American Indian
7. Staten Island Ferry

Seeing the sights in New York is often just a matter of turning the corner. "Ballet aerialists" dangling from the Stock Exchange, brass bands wailing at Chinatown street funerals, and wall-to-wall "hot dogs" preening during Dachshund Day in Washington Square Park—you won't pay a penny for any of it. Here are some other free (or dirt-cheap) ways to savor the Big Apple. START: **Subway 6 to 77th or 86th Street.**

❶ ★★ Summer Music in Central Park. The **New York Philharmonic** plays free evening concerts on the Great Lawn (midpark from 79th–85th sts.; http://nyphil.org). Nearby, **Shakespeare in the Park** features free, star-studded Public Theater productions of Shakespeare classics in June at the Delacorte Theater (southwest corner of the Great Lawn, midpark at 80th St.; www.publictheater.org).

❷ ★★ Roosevelt Island Tram and FDR Four Freedoms Park. Roosevelt Island residents who ride the tram back and forth to Manhattan every day are privy to one of New York's best-kept secrets: The view from the tram is one of the city's most dramatic. Look down the East River during the 4-minute ride, and you'll see four bridges (Queensboro, Williamsburg, Manhattan, and Brooklyn). On Roosevelt Island, explore calming Franklin D.

The Philharmonic playing in Central Park.

Roosevelt Four Freedoms Park. Designed by acclaimed architect Louis Kahn, the park was commissioned in 1973 by then-mayor John Lindsay as a tribute to FDR. Soon after the announcement, Kahn died unexpectedly, New York went bankrupt, and the park became just a pipe dream. But the dream became a reality 39 years later when the memorial finally opened to the public in October 2012. The centerpiece of the park is a 1,050-pound bronze bust of Roosevelt by sculptor Jo Davidson. *Closed Tuesdays. Tram at Second Ave. & 59th St. Fare $2.50. Subway: 4/5/6/N/R/W to 59th St.*

❸ ★★★ New York Public Library. This magnificent Beaux Arts building, worth a trip in itself, has permanent and temporary exhibitions plus a nice gift shop in the lobby. Oh, and it's all free. *See p 30.*

❹ ★ Movies in Bryant Park. During most of the year, Bryant

The Roosevelt Island tram.

A mask from the National Museum of the American Indian.

Park is a peaceful oasis of green, just behind the New York Public Library. In summer, though, the park hosts its Summer Film Festival featuring classic-movie screenings on Monday evenings at dusk. The lawn opens at 5pm for blankets and picnics. *Bordered by 40th & 42nd sts. & Fifth & Sixth aves.* ☎ *212/512-5700. www.bryantpark.org. Subway: B/D/F/M to 42nd St.*

⑤ ★★ High Line. A derelict elevated freight-train track has been reborn as an inspired public park, which winds along pathways through an outdoor "integrative landscape" of natural habitats and art installations alongside stunning Hudson River views. *See p 4.*

⑥ ★★ kids National Museum of the American Indian. This Smithsonian Institution museum houses a fabulous collection of artifacts in the Cass Gilbert–designed Alexander Hamilton U.S. Custom House, one of the city's most impressive buildings—and it's free! *See p 53.*

⑦ ★★ Staten Island Ferry. This free 25-minute ride takes you up close and past the Statue of Liberty and Ellis Island. *Whitehall Ferry Terminal.* ☎ *718/727-2508. www. siferry.com.* ●

TV Tapings

It's free—but not easy—to view the tapings of such New York–based shows as *The Late Show with David Letterman, The Colbert Report, The Daily Show with Jon Stewart, The Rachel Ray Show,* and *The View*. The catch is ordering tickets well in advance. Check the "ticket request" section on each show's website and specify how many tickets you want and your preferred dates. For the latest details, go to the website of **NYC & Company,** the city's official marketing and tourism department (☎ 212/484-1222; www.nycgo. com), and check out "TV Show Tapings."

The Metropolitan Museum of Art

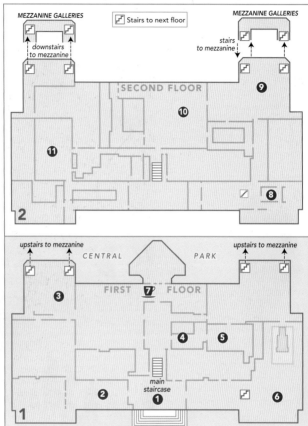

MEZZANINE GALLERIES

Stairs to next floor

MEZZANINE GALLERIES

downstairs to mezzanine

stairs to mezzanine

SECOND FLOOR

9

10

11

8

2

upstairs to mezzanine

CENTRAL   PARK

upstairs to mezzanine

3

FIRST **7** FLOOR

4   **5**

main staircase

2

1

6

1

MAIN ENTRANCE
Fifth Avenue

1. The Great Hall
2. Greek & Roman Galleries
3. Modern Art Wing
4. European Sculpture & Decorative Arts
5. Arms & Armor
6. Egyptian Art
7. Cafeteria
8. Asian Art
9. American Wing
10. European Paintings: Old Masters
11. European Paintings: 19th & Early 20th Centuries

Previous page: Inside the Museum of Modern Art.

In 1866, a group of New Yorkers decided their hometown needed a museum that would function as a living encyclopedia of world art. Today, the Metropolitan Museum of Art and the associated Cloisters museums fulfill that promise with a collection of more than two million objects dating from the Paleolithic period—that is, the Stone Age—to the early 21st century.

① The Great Hall. The main entrance to the Met makes all who enter feel like royalty. With its soaring ceilings, elegant balconies, and restrained use of Greco-Roman motifs, it's a fine example of neoclassical architecture. The massive sprays of fresh flowers have been a tradition here since 1969.

② ★★★ Greek & Roman Galleries. Some 3,700 people per day have visited the spectacular Greek and Roman galleries since their opening in 2007. The centerpiece is the **Leon Levy and Shelby White Court,** a dramatic peristyle area rich with Hellenistic and Roman art. Among its treasures is a massive statue of **Hercules** with a lion skin draped heroically over his arm. In the galleries, visitors can see **Roman frescoes** long buried under ash after a volcanic eruption; exquisite **gold serpentine armbands;** and the **"Black Bedroom,"** reputedly made for a villa built by a close friend of the Emperor Augustus.

③ ★★ Modern Art Wing. Head through the galleries of the

The Met's Great Hall.

Arts of Africa, Oceania, and the Americas to get to the Modern Art Wing, which is full of blockbuster works. Must-sees include **Pablo Picasso's** *Gertrude Stein,* **Jackson Pollock's** *Autumn Rhythm,* and **Edward Hopper's** *The Lighthouse at Two Lights.*

Practical Matters

The Met (☎ 212/535-7710; www.metmuseum.org; Sun–Thurs 10am–5:30pm; Fri–Sat 10am–9pm) is located at 1000 Fifth Ave. (at 82nd St.). Admission is $25 adults, $17 seniors, $12 students, and free for children under 12 with adult. If you're in a rush, skip the main entrance on 82nd and enter through 81st Street. The least crowded times are Friday and Saturday nights or right at opening time.

❹ ★★ **European Sculpture & Decorative Arts.** These galleries are filled with period rooms that include a handsome bedroom from an 18th-century **Venetian palace** and a mid-18th-century **Tapestry Room** from an English country estate. Especially astonishing is the *Studiolo* from the Ducal Palace in Gubbio: The walls of this small Renaissance study are covered in elaborate *trompe l'oeil* panels inlaid with thousands of pieces of wood to give the illusion of a room lined with cabinets containing books, musical instruments, and scientific tools.

❺ ★ kids **Arms & Armor.** The full sets of European armor in the courtyard are dazzling, but make sure to pop into the smaller galleries that surround the court. Here you'll find such curiosities as ceremonial saddles carved from bone and pistols inlaid with semiprecious stones. A Turkish saber created in 1876 for the investiture of an Ottoman sultan (who had a nervous breakdown before the ceremony and was deposed) is a miracle of sparkling diamonds, smooth-as-ice jade, and rich gold.

❻ ★★★ kids **Egyptian Art.** The **Temple of Dendur,** built in 15 B.C. and relocated from Egypt, is arguably the most famous object at the Met. Inside, you'll find graffiti from Victorian-era travelers. For a glimpse of daily life in ancient Egypt, check out the 13 wooden models from the **tomb of Meketre.** These models represent the nobleman's earthly wealth that is to be taken with him into the afterlife. They show his bakery, his dairy, his beer-producing facility, and boats.

❼ **Cafeteria.** Year-round you can grab a good, filling lunch at the Met's ground-floor cafeteria ($)—it even has kids' meals. Or, if it's a

The Cloisters

If you still have energy after visiting the Met, hop on the M4 bus at Madison and 83rd Street and head 8 miles uptown to **The Cloisters** (☎ 212/923-3700). This museum devoted to medieval art and architecture is a branch of the Met, but it feels like a world apart. In Fort Tryon Park overlooking the Hudson, the building incorporates elements from five medieval monasteries in France, Spain, and Italy.

Besides The Cloisters' magnificent setting and extraordinary architecture, it would be worth coming just to see *The Unicorn Tapestries,* a series of seven tapestries depicting a sometimes brutal hunt that ends with the resurrection of the unicorn enclosed in a garden under a pomegranate tree. Robert Campin's ***Annunciation*** altarpiece is another memorable work. Filled with genre details, it depicts the Virgin Mary in a medieval Dutch setting.

Note: The last stop on the M4 is directly in front of The Cloisters. The ride takes 1 hour. Admission is free with same-day Met sticker.

nice day, head outside the main entrance and get a snack from one of the carts ($) on the plaza. The food won't be gourmet, but eating a pretzel or hot dog while people-watching from the steps of the museum is a quintessential New York experience. For other dining options, see p 34.

⑧ ★ Asian Art. The **Astor Court,** a Chinese scholar's garden based on a Ming Dynasty design, is a great place for a little R&R. The principle of yin and yang, or opposites, gives this space its sense of harmony and tranquility—that, and it's often inexplicably deserted. Also in this section: the Japanese galleries, filled with delicate scrolls, screens, kimonos, and tapestries. And don't miss the **Japanese tearoom/study room.**

⑨ ★★ American Wing. This airy, light-filled section of the Met is a museum inside a museum. The Hudson River School paintings are extraordinary in their scope, from the grandeur of **Frederick Church's** *The Heart of the Andes* to the delicate and refined *Lake George* by **John Kensett.** Plenty is recognizable here, from the iconic *Washington Crossing the Delaware* by **Emanuel Leutze** to **John Singer Sargent's** *Madame X* to **Winslow Homer's** *Northeaster.* The American Wing includes 25 furnished period rooms from the late 17th to the early 20th centuries, including **Frank Lloyd Wright's** *Living Room from the Little House.*

⑩ ★★ European Paintings: Old Masters. To get to these galleries, cross the Engelhard Court and go up the elegant Louis Sullivan staircase to the second level. As you open the door into the European paintings galleries, you'll come face to face with

Francisco José de Goya's Majas on a Balcony.

Rembrandt's *Aristotle with a Bust of Homer.* Other highlights include **Vermeer**'s *Young Woman with a Water Jug,* **El Greco**'s *Portrait of a Cardinal,* **Velázquez**'s *Juan de Pareja,* **Goya**'s *Don Manuel,* and **Duccio**'s *Madonna and Child.*

⑪ ★★★ European Paintings: 19th & Early 20th Centuries. One of the most popular sections in the museum, these galleries include a good sampling of Impressionist art. Here you can compare **Gustave Courbet**'s controversial and explicitly sexual *Woman with a Parrot* with a more discreet version by **Edouard Manet.** Finally, take a look at **Paul Cézanne**'s *Still Life with Apples and Pears* with its funky perspectives and innovative use of color to get a feel for the radical changes in painting that developed in the 20th century.

⑫ The Costume Institute. This favorite of fashionistas features more than 35,000 costumes and accessories from all over the world, spanning from the 15th century to the present. Currently under renovation, the Costume Institute is due to reopen sometime in 2014.

The Best Small Museums

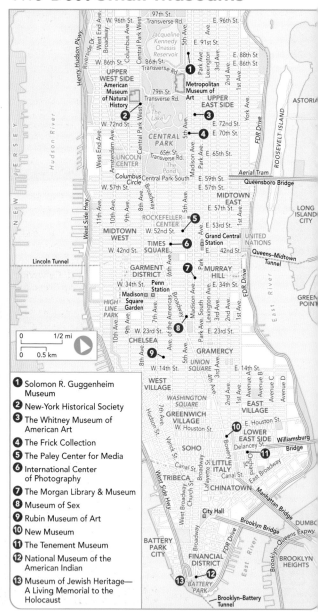

1. Solomon R. Guggenheim Museum
2. New-York Historical Society
3. The Whitney Museum of American Art
4. The Frick Collection
5. The Paley Center for Media
6. International Center of Photography
7. The Morgan Library & Museum
8. Museum of Sex
9. Rubin Museum of Art
10. New Museum
11. The Tenement Museum
12. National Museum of the American Indian
13. Museum of Jewish Heritage—A Living Memorial to the Holocaust

Few cities can match New York in the breadth and depth of its museum collections. Sure, the big boys are here—the Met, MoMA, and the Natural History museum—but world-class treasures await in the smaller collections as well. Here are some of the best to get you started. You would need at least 3 days to see all these. *Note:* Many museums offer free admission Friday evenings; check their websites to see.

❶ ★★★ Solomon R. Guggenheim Museum. One of the largest of New York's small museums, the Guggenheim holds a wide-ranging collection of modern art, from an 1867 landscape by Camille Pissaro to important works by Picasso, Kandinsky, and Modigliani. The building alone is a masterpiece, a project that took Frank Lloyd Wright 15 years to fully imagine. *See p 40.*

❷ ★★ New-York Historical Society. The New-York Historical Society is a major repository of American history, culture, and art, with a special focus on New York. Where else can you find a collection that includes Tiffany lamps, vintage dollhouses, Audubon watercolors, life and death masks of prominent Americans, and even George Washington's camp bed? ⏱ 1½ hr. 2 W. 77th St. (at Central Park West). ☎ 212/873-3400. www. nyhistory.org. Admission $15 adults, $12 seniors, $10 students, free for children 12 & under. Tues–Sat 10am–6pm (till 8pm Fri), Sun 11am–5pm. Bus: M79. Subway: 1 to 79th St.

❸ ★★ The Whitney Museum of American Art. This museum was built around Gertrude Vanderbilt Whitney's collection of 20th-century art, including works by Edward Hopper, Jasper Johns, and Georgia O'Keefe. The original museum was established in 1931 near Vanderbilt's home in Greenwich Village. It has been in its present home, a concrete-and-granite structure designed by architect Marcel Breuer, since 1966. The collection includes provocative 21st-century pieces, many of them shown in the trend-setting Whitney Biennial, an exhibition of cutting-edge works by up-and-coming artists. ⏱ 2 hr. 945 Madison Ave. (at 75th St.). ☎ 800/WHITNEY (944-8639). http://whitney.org. Admission $20 adults, $16 seniors & students, free for children 18 & under. Wed–Thurs & Sat–Sun 11am–6pm, Fri 1–9pm. Subway: 6 to 77th St.

❹ ★★★ The Frick Collection. If you want to see how Gilded Age millionaires lived, don't miss the Frick. It's said that steel titan Henry Clay Frick commissioned this marble mansion to make his fellow industrialist Andrew Carnegie's home "look like a miner's shack." The collection is first-rate, with period rooms hung with works by

The Whitney Museum of American Art.

Rembrandt, Goya, Vermeer, James McNeill Whistler, Jean Baptiste Camille Corot, and Frederick Turner. See p 25.

5 ★ kids The Paley Center for Media. Formerly known as the **Museum of Television & Radio,** this interactive museum is irresistible fun. You can see performances by great personalities past and present—from Milton Berle to Jerry Seinfeld—or do your own computer search of the museum's nearly 150,000 TV and radio shows and ads you half-remember from childhood. History buffs can revisit great moments, such as the dismantling of the Berlin Wall. ⏱ 1½ hr. 25 W. 52nd St. (btw. Fifth & Sixth aves.). ☎ 212/621-6600. www.paleycenter. org. Admission $10 adults, $8 seniors & students, $5 for children 14 & under. Wed & Fri–Sun noon–6pm, Thurs noon–8pm. Subway: B/D/F/M to 47th–50th sts.

6 ★ International Center of Photography. A must-see for any photography buff, the ICP is one of the world's premier educators, collectors, and exhibitors of photographic art. The collection includes 50,000-plus prints with an emphasis on contemporary photographic works, but with a respectable collection of historically important photographers as well. ⏱ 1 hr. 1133 Sixth Ave. (at 43rd St.). ☎ 212/857-0000. www.icp.org. Admission $14 adults, $10 seniors & students, free for children 12 & under. Tues–Thurs & Sat–Sun 10am–6pm, Fri 10am–8pm. Subway: B/D/F/M to 42nd St.

7 ★★ The Morgan Library & Museum. This Italian Renaissance–style mansion—once the private library of financier Pierpont Morgan—boasts one of the best collections of rare books and manuscripts in the world. Look for the autographed manuscript of a Mozart

symphony, early children's books, a chalk drawing by Peter Paul Rubens, and the ornate illustrations in medieval and Renaissance manuscripts. ⏱ 2 hr. 225 Madison Ave. (at 36th St.). ☎ 212/685-0610. www.the morgan.org. Admission $18 adults; $12 seniors, students & children 13–16; free for children 12 & under. Tues–Thurs 10:30am–5pm, Fri 10:30am–9pm, Sat 10am–6pm, Sun 11am–6pm. Subway: B/D/F/N/Q/R/M to 34th St.

8 ★ Museum of Sex. When this museum opened in 2002, it managed to cause a stir even among hard-bitten New Yorkers. Among the collections are early sex films, artifacts from burlesque theaters, S&M displays, painted nudes, and even blow-up dolls. ⏱ 1 hr. 233 Fifth Ave. (at 27th St.). ☎ 866/MOSEX-NYC (667-3969). www. museumofsex.com. Admission $18 adults, $15 students & seniors. No one under 18 admitted. Sun–Thurs 10am–8pm, Fri–Sat 10am–9pm. Subway: N/R to 28th St.

9 ★★ Rubin Museum of Art. New York must have some good karma: In October 2004, it scored this stunning collection of Himalayan art. In the former Chelsea outpost of Barneys, the Rubin Museum features sculptures, paintings, and textiles. Great gift shop, too. ⏱ 1½ hr. 150 W. 17th St. (btw. Sixth & Seventh aves.). ☎ 212/620-5000. www. rmanyc.org. Admission $10 adults; $5 seniors, students & artists; free for children 12 & under. Mon & Thurs 11am–5pm, Wed 11am–7pm, Fri 11am–10pm, Sat–Sun 11am–6pm. Subway: 1/9 to 18th St.

10 ★ New Museum. The seven stories of the New Museum of contemporary art, designed by Tokyo–based architects Kazuyo Sejima and Ryue Nishizawa (aka SANAA), rise above the tenement buildings of the Lower East Side like boxes haphazardly piled upon one another.

The offbeat exterior reflects the character of the exhibitions inside by new and emerging artists.
🕐 1 hr. 235 Bowery (at Prince St.). ☎ 212/219-1222. www.newmuseum. org. Admission $14 adults, $12 seniors, $10 students, free for children 18 & under; free for all Thurs 7–9pm. Wed & Fri–Sun 11am–6pm; Thurs 11am–9pm. Subway: 6 to Spring St.; N/R to Prince St.

⓫ ★★★ kids The Tenement Museum. Conceived as a monument to the experience of "urban pioneers" in America, this don't-miss museum documents the lives of immigrant residents in a six-story tenement built in 1863 at 97 Orchard St. (accessible only via the highly recommended guided tours). The tenement rooms are eerily authentic, and for good reason: 97 Orchard was essentially boarded up from 1935 to 1987; when it was finally opened, everything was exactly as it had been left in 1935, a virtual time capsule of tenement life. Artifacts found range from the mundane (medicine tins and Russian cigarettes) to the personal (a 1922 Ouija board and an infant's

The New Museum.

button-up shoe). Among several tours to choose from, the living-history **Meet Victoria Confino tour** tells of the hardscrabble life that many immigrants faced in the late 19th and early 20th centuries. Book your visit online at least a week in advance—this is one of New York's most popular museums. 🕐 1–1½ hr. 103 Orchard St. (at Delancey St.). ☎ 212/982-8420. www.tenement. org. Tours $22 adults, $17 seniors & students. Tours daily.

⓬ ★★ kids National Museum of the American Indian. In 1626, regional tribes sold Manhattan Island to the Dutch West India Company for 60 guilders. This museum's fascinating collection of artifacts spans that period as well as more than 10,000 years of North and South America's pre-European history. 🕐 1 hr. 1 Bowling Green. ☎ 212/514-3700. www.nmai.si.edu. Free admission. Daily 10am–5pm (Thurs till 8pm). Subway: 4/5 to Bowling Green; 1/9 to South Ferry.

⓭ ★★ Museum of Jewish Heritage—A Living Memorial to the Holocaust. Dedicated to teaching people of all backgrounds about 20th-century Jewish life, this award-winning museum was designed in a six-sided shape to symbolize the Star of David and to honor the six million Jews who died in the Holocaust. Inside are photos, artifacts, and moving accounts from survivors. A second-story stone garden—where each of the hollowed-out boulders has a tree growing out of it—overlooks New York Harbor. 🕐 2 hr. 36 Battery Place. ☎ 646/437-4200. www.mjhnyc.org. Admission $12 adults, $10 seniors, $7 students, free for children 12 & under. Sun–Tues & Thurs 10am–5:45pm, Wed 10am–8pm, Fri 10am–5pm, eves of Jewish holidays 10am–3pm. Subway: 4/5 to Bowling Green; 1 to South Ferry.

The American Museum of Natural History

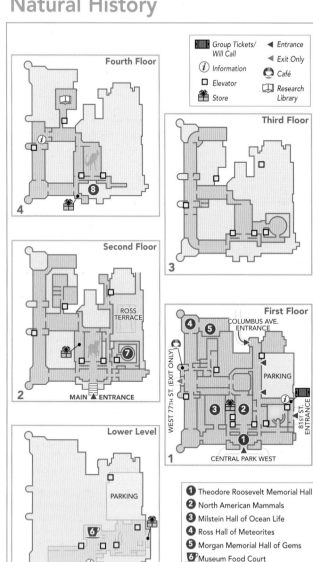

Fourth Floor

4

Group Tickets/Will Call
(i) Information
Elevator
Store

◄ Entrance
◄ Exit Only
Café
Research Library

Third Floor

3

Second Floor

ROSS TERRACE

7

MAIN ENTRANCE

2

8

First Floor

4 5
COLUMBUS AVE. ENTRANCE

WEST 77TH ST. (EXIT ONLY)

PARKING

81ST ST. ENTRANCE

3 2

1

CENTRAL PARK WEST

1

Lower Level

PARKING

6

81 St. Subway Station (B-C)

LL

1 Theodore Roosevelt Memorial Hall
2 North American Mammals
3 Milstein Hall of Ocean Life
4 Ross Hall of Meteorites
5 Morgan Memorial Hall of Gems
6 Museum Food Court
7 Rose Center for Earth & Science/Hayden Planetarium
8 Koch Dinosaur Wing

It's got dinosaurs, giant sapphires, and towering totem poles—and that's just for starters. The American Museum of Natural History has one of the most diverse and thrilling collections in the world—four floors of natural wonders and cultural artifacts for the intrepid explorer in all of us. It's delicious fun for every age.

1 ★★ Theodore Roosevelt Memorial Hall. The sight of a giant *Barosaurus* fossil in this soaring entrance rotunda provides a smashing introduction to the rest of your visit.

2 ★★ North American Mammals. One of the museum's popular Habitat Group Dioramas, where skillfully mounted animals are shown in lifelike reproductions of their natural habitats. In one diorama, an Alaskan brown bear, the world's largest living land carnivore, rears up on its hind legs.

3 ★★ Milstein Hall of Ocean Life. This vast first-floor room explores life in the deep blue sea, with lighted fish dioramas and a spectacular replica of a giant blue whale overhead.

4 ★★ Ross Hall of Meteorites. On display is a 34-ton meteorite, said to be merely a fragment of a massive meteorite that scientists estimate weighed around 200 tons.

5 ★ Morgan Memorial Hall of Gems. This collection of precious gems includes the biggest sapphire ever found, the 563-carat Star of India.

6 Museum Food Court. Sustenance for the whole family, including barbecue, paninis, and sandwiches. *Lower level. $–$$.*

7 ★★★ Rose Center for Earth & Space/Hayden Planetarium. A sphere inside a seven-story glass cube holds the Hayden Planetarium, where you can take a virtual ride through the Milky Way. Prepare to be blown away by the planetarium **Space Show.** Buy your tickets in advance for the Space Show to guarantee admission (they're available online).

8 ★★★ Koch Dinosaur Wing. The fourth floor contains the largest collection of real dinosaur fossils in the world. Among the treasures is the *Tyrannosaurus rex,* with 6-inch-long teeth, and the first *Velociraptor* skull ever found.

Practical Matters

The **AMNH** (☎ 212/769-5100; www.amnh.org; daily 10am–5:45pm) is on Central Park West (btw. 77th and 81st sts.). Admission (includes entrance to Rose Center, above) is $22 adults, $17 seniors and students, $13 children 2 to 12; Space Show (see above) and museum admission is $27 adults, $22 seniors and students, $16 children 2 to 12. You'll need about 4 hours to see the whole thing. Buy tickets in advance for specific IMAX shows or special exhibitions.

The Museum of Modern Art

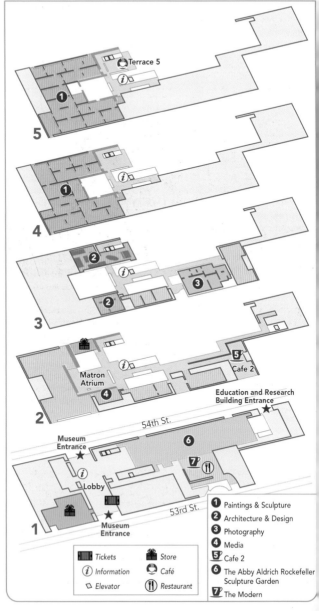

Terrace 5

5 ❶

❶ 4

❷ ❷ ❸ 3

🎁 Matron Atrium ❹ 2

🎁 5️⃣ Cafe 2

Education and Research
Building Entrance ★

54th St.

Museum
Entrance ★

ℹ️

Lobby

❻

7️⃣ 🍴

53rd St.

Museum
Entrance ★

🎟️ Tickets	🎁 Store
ℹ️ Information	☕ Café
🛗 Elevator	🍴 Restaurant

❶ Paintings & Sculpture
❷ Architecture & Design
❸ Photography
❹ Media
5️⃣ Cafe 2
❻ The Abby Aldrich Rockefeller
   Sculpture Garden
7️⃣ The Modern

For the best in modern painting and sculpture from the late 19th century to the present, head straight to MoMA, as it's affectionately known. The 2006 renovation by Yoshio Taniguchi highlights space and light, with open rooms, high ceilings, and gardens. It's a beautiful work of architecture that complements the art within—a vast repository also encompassing drawings, photographs, architectural models and modern furniture, iconic design objects ranging from tableware to sports cars, and film and video.

Studying Barnett Newman's Vir Heroicus Sublimis *at the Museum of Modern Art.*

① ★★★ **Painting & Sculpture.** Start your tour at the top: on the fourth and fifth floors. Among the museum treasures are **Vincent van Gogh**'s *The Starry Night,* **Paul Cézanne**'s *The Bather,* **Picasso**'s *Les Demoiselles d'Avignon,* and **Henri Rousseau**'s *The Sleeping Gypsy.* Look for celebrated works by Henri Matisse, Paul Gauguin, Marc Chagall, Edward Hopper, René Magritte, Willem de Kooning, Mark Rothko, Barnett Newman, Frank Stella, and Jackson Pollock.

② ★★★ **Architecture & Design.** The third floor contains some 28,000 works that perhaps more than any other collection reflect the form-follows-function dynamism of the modern era. Here are Eames chairs, Frank Lloyd Wright windows, a 1908 Peter Behrens fan, and even elegantly designed ball bearings.

Practical Matters

The **MoMA** (☎ 212/708-9400; www.moma.org; Sat–Thurs 10:30am–5:30pm, Fri 10:30am–8pm) is at 11 W. 53rd St. (btw. Fifth and Sixth aves.). Admission is $25 adults, $18 seniors, $14 students, and free for kids 16 and under when accompanied by an adult. You'll need a full day to see it all.

❸ ★★ Photography. MoMA started collecting photographs in 1930, well before most people considered photography an art form. This stunning collection on the third floor holds important works by Walker Evans, Man Ray, and Cindy Sherman, as well as mid-19th-century albumen silver prints from glass-plate negatives.

Travel Tip

MoMA's museum-wide Wi-Fi network allows visitors to access the museum's mobile website on smartphones and tablets. Audio tours and commentary can be found there; content is available in eight languages and in specialized versions for children, teenagers, and the visually impaired.

❹ ★ Media. This collection on the second floor covers some 50 years of works in media, from moving-image installations and short films to pieces that combine avant-garde performance art and video.

❺ ★ Cafe 2. Forget the museum cafes of old, with rubbery food and harsh lighting. This museum cafe has a soft wood-and-gold shimmer and serves handmade pastas, artisanal cheeses, seasonal soups, paninis, and decent wines. *2nd floor. $–$$.*

❻ ★★ Abby Aldrich Rockefeller Sculpture Garden. This landscaped outdoor space (originally designed by architect Philip Johnson) is home to works of sculpture from the museum collection. Look for **Picasso**'s whimsical *She-Goat* (1950) and **Alberto Giacometti**'s long, lean *Tall Figure III* (1960) as well as installations by contemporary artists, such as **Richard Serra.**

❼ ★★ The Modern. Whether you're here for lunch, dinner, or a cocktail, this is a destination in itself. It's sleek and fabulous, with big glass windows overlooking the sculpture garden. *1st floor.* ☎ *212/333-1220. www.themodern nyc.com. $$$.* ●

P.S. 1 Contemporary Art Center

If you're interested in new work that's thrillingly cutting-edge, this MoMA affiliate is worth the trip—one stop outside Manhattan in Queens. Originally a public school, **P.S. 1** (22–25 Jackson Ave. at 46th Ave., Long Island City; ☎ 718/784-2084; www.ps1.org; Thurs–Mon noon–6pm) is one of the country's largest nonprofit art institutions, exhibiting contemporary art from America and abroad. The array of works includes large-scale exhibitions by such artists as James Turrell and Richard Serra. Almost as enticing as the art are the innovative dishes found at the museum's restaurant, **M. Wells Dinette** (☎ 718/786-1800; $). Admission to P.S. 1 is $10 adults, $5 seniors and students. Take the E or M train to 23rd Street/Ely Avenue, or the 7 train to 45th Road/Court House Square.

The Best **Neighborhood** Walks

Downtown & New York Harbor

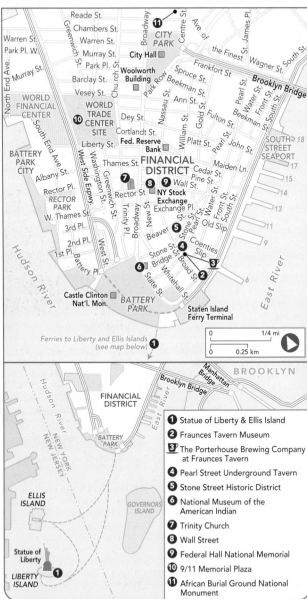

0 — 1/4 mi
0 — 0.25 km

Ferries to Liberty and Ellis Islands
(see map below) ❶

BROOKLYN

1 Statue of Liberty & Ellis Island

2 Fraunces Tavern Museum

3² The Porterhouse Brewing Company
at Fraunces Tavern

4 Pearl Street Underground Tavern

5 Stone Street Historic District

6 National Museum of the
American Indian

7 Trinity Church

8 Wall Street

9 Federal Hall National Memorial

10 9/11 Memorial Plaza

11 African Burial Ground National
Monument

Previous page: A brownstone in Park Slope, Brooklyn.

The southern tip of Manhattan is where the action began some 400 years ago. This area includes 17th-century cobblestone alleyways, the seaport where 18th-century commerce helped build the city, historic landmarks of the American Revolution, and the canyons of Wall Street, constructed in outsize Deco style in the early 20th century.

❶ ★★★ kids Statue of Liberty. Annie Moore, an Irish teenager, celebrated her 15th birthday on January 1, 1892, as the first person to pass through Ellis Island, America's main point of entry for immigrants from 1892 to 1954. For Annie and the 12 million others who subsequently entered the U.S. by way of Ellis Island, Lady Liberty was likely their first glimpse of America. The statue was created to commemorate 100 years of American independence in 1876. But it wasn't until 1886 that the statue was finally dedicated on U.S. soil. On Liberty Island, you can explore the **Statue of Liberty Museum,** peer into the inner structure through a glass ceiling near the base of the statue, enjoy views from the observation deck atop a 16-story pedestal, and now climb to the crown for a panoramic view of downtown. (At press time, **Ellis Island** was closed due to damage inflicted by Hurricane Sandy in 2012.) ⏱ *1 hr. See p 18.*

❷ Fraunces Tavern Museum. It was on this site that George Washington bade farewell to his officers at the end of the American Revolution with these words: "With a heart full of love and gratitude I now take leave of you. I most devoutly wish that your latter days may be as prosperous and happy as your former ones have been glorious and honorable." The museum here (in the 1907 replica of the original 1717 tavern) has period rooms, art and artifacts (including a

The Fraunces Tavern Museum.

lock of Washington's hair and one of his false teeth), and temporary exhibits. ⏱ *45 min. 54 Pearl St. (near Broad St.).* ☎ *212/425-1778. www.frauncestavernmuseum.org. Admission $7 adults, $4 seniors, students & children 6–18, free for children 5 & under. Daily noon–5pm. Subway: R/W to Whitehall St.; 4/5 to Bowling Green; 1 to South Ferry.*

❸ The Porterhouse Brewing Company at Fraunces Tavern. Housed in the museum, this Irish brewery/restaurant serves lunch and dinner with an emphasis on Colonial-era vittles (steamed mussels, oysters, and shepherd's pie). *54 Pearl St. (near Broad St.).* ☎ *212/968-1776. $$.*

Choir practice at Trinity Church.

④ ★ Lovelace Tavern Site. Little is left of 17th-century New York, but an excavation in 1979 led to the discovery of the foundation of Lovelace Tavern, built in 1670. In an ingenious move, the underground excavation was left in place—as was an early-18th-century cistern—and the sidewalk above it was replaced with Plexiglas, so that anyone walking by can look down and see the old foundation and artifacts. *Pearl St. at Coenties Alley. Subway: R/W to Whitehall St.; 4/5 to Bowling Green, 1/9 to South Ferry.*

⑤ ★★ Stone Street Historic District. This 17th-century cobblestone alley has become a mini–dining-and-drinking enclave, with restaurants, bars, and a heralded pizzeria. *See p 62.*

⑥ ★★ kids National Museum of the American Indian. Set inside one of the city's most extravagant Beaux Arts landmarks—the 1907 Alexander Hamilton U.S. Custom House—this small Smithsonian museum's collection spans more than 10,000 years of North and South America's pre-European history. The Cass Gilbert building is awfully grand, with marine motifs, voluminous columns, an elliptical rotunda, and marble aplenty.

What's more, admission is free. *See p 53.*

⑦ ★★ Trinity Church. Alexander Hamilton is buried in the church's south cemetery. The original building was erected in 1698, although the present structure dates from 1846. *See p 17.*

⑧ ★★★ Wall Street. The street synonymous with high finance began, literally, in 1653 as a 12-foot-high (3.6m) wooden palisade built by the Dutch to keep out the British. Today, it's home to some of the city's most magnificent architecture, skyscraping Jazz Age marvels made all the more impressive by the narrowness of the streets. Check out the BNY Mellon Building, **1 Wall St.,** a tiered limestone Art Deco gem built in 1931. In 1920, a bomb exploded in front of **23 Wall St.**—then the headquarters of J. P. Morgan—killing 38 people and injuring 400; it was said to be the work of anarchists. Farther down the block at **40 Wall St.** is a building that was for a nanosecond the tallest in the world; the 1930 Deco beauty was soon overtaken in height by the Chrysler Building. The sumptuous Merchants' Exchange (now Cipriani Wall Street) at **55 Wall St.** was built in 1842 but was added onto by McKim, Meade & White in 1907. *Wall St. (btw. Broadway & FDR Dr.).*

9 ★ **Federal Hall National Memorial.** This majestic 1842 structure is one of Wall Street's most recognizable monuments. On this site, the First Congress met and the Bill of Rights was written. It was out in front that George Washington was inaugurated, on April 30, 1789 (right where his statue stands today). The capital moved to Philadelphia in 1790, and the original Federal Hall was torn down in 1812. ⏱ *15 min. 26 Wall St. (btw. Nassau & William sts.).* ☎ *212/825-6888. www.nps.gov/feha. Free admission. Mon–Fri 9am–5pm. Subway: 2/3/4/5/6 to Wall St.*

10 ★★★ **9/11 Memorial Plaza.** Encompassing an 8-acre (3.2-ha) plaza, the centerpiece of

this moving tribute to those who perished in the September 11, 2001, terrorist attacks is the two reflecting pools and waterfalls located in the footprints of where the Twin Towers stood. *See p 16.*

11 **African Burial Ground National Monument.** During construction of an office tower here in 1991, masses of human remains were unearthed. Research revealed that the area was a burial ground for slaves and freedmen. The site was designated a National Historic Landmark, and in 2007 a granite memorial was built to pay tribute to the estimated 15,000 Africans and African Americans who were buried here. *Duane & Elk sts. Visitor center at 290 Broadway.* ☎ *212/637-2019. www.nps.gov/afbg. Daily 9am–5pm (till 4pm in winter); visitor center and indoor exhibitions Tues–Sat 10am–4pm. Free admission.*

The Best **Neighborhood Walks**

Historic **Harlem**

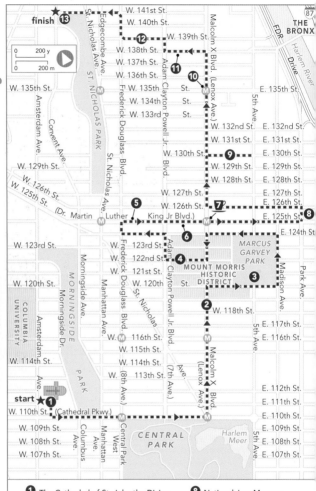

1. The Cathedral of St. John the Divine
2. Mount Morris Park Historic District
3. Marcus Garvey Park
4. Hale House Center
5. Apollo Theater
6. Studio Museum in Harlem
7. Red Rooster Harlem
8. National Jazz Museum in Harlem
9. Astor Row
10. Schomburg Center for Research in Black Culture
11. Abyssinian Baptist Church
12. Strivers' Row
13. Hamilton Grange

It wasn't until the mid–19th century that Nieuw Amsterdam and Nieuw Haarlem—the two towns the Dutch founded on the island of Manhattan—became one. But Harlem, largely shaped by African Americans who came north in droves after the Civil War and again after the end of World War I, has retained its own distinct character to this day.

① ★★★ The Cathedral of St. John the Divine. The mother church of New York's Episcopal diocese makes a good starting point for your walk. If it is ever completed, it will be the largest Gothic-style cathedral in the world. The land was purchased in 1887, the cornerstone was laid in 1892, and the choir was finally installed in 1911. Work stopped with the advent of World War II and then resumed in 1979. St. John the Divine houses fantastic art treasures in its thematic chapels (dedicated to sports, poetry, and firefighting, among other subjects). Above the choir, the 17th-century **Barberini Tapestries** depict scenes from the life of Christ. The tremendous rose window comprises 10,000 pieces of colored glass. ⏱ *45 min. 1047 Amsterdam Ave. (btw. 111th & 112th sts.).* ☎ *212/316-7490. www.stjohndivine.org. Public tours $6 adults, $5 students & seniors. Daily 7:30am–6pm. Subway: 1/9 to 110th St.*

② ★★ Mount Morris Park Historic District. This impressively preserved collection of handsome 19th- and 20th-century row houses and brownstones features various styles, from Romanesque Revival to Queen Anne. *Bounded by 119th St., 124th St., Lenox Ave. & Mount Morris Park West.*

③ ★ Marcus Garvey Park. Centered on a rocky outcropping that is one of the highest natural points on Manhattan, the park was renamed in 1973 in honor of black nationalist leader Marcus Garvey.

The elaborate front facade of St. John the Divine.

(Firefighters built a watchtower here in 1865; alas, the top is now closed to visitors.) *120th St. & Mount Morris Park West.*

④ Hale House Center. Established in 1969 by Mother Clara Hale to aid drug-addicted infants and their mothers, Hale House is now a learning center for children and families. Hale died in 1992, but sculptor Robert Berks memorialized her in a sculpture surrounded by etched bronze plaques of children. *152 W. 122nd St. (btw. Seventh Ave. & Malcolm X Blvd.).*

⑤ ★★★ Apollo Theater. This legendary venue has featured them all—Count Basie, Billie Holiday, Louis Armstrong, Duke Ellington, Marvin Gaye, Aretha Franklin, B. B. King, and more. "Amateur Night at the Apollo" launched the careers of

Ella Fitzgerald, James Brown, Lauryn Hill, and the Jackson 5—and it's still going strong. Historic tours are generally scheduled for groups and must be booked well in advance. *253 W. 125th St. (Frederick Douglass Blvd.). ☎ 212/531-5300. www.apollotheater.org. Amateur Night tickets $19–$40. Tours $14 weekdays, $16 weekends. Subway: A/B/C/D/2/3 to 125th St.*

6 ★ Studio Museum in Harlem. Since 1968, the SMH has been devoted to collecting, preserving, and promoting 19th- and 20th-century African-American art as well as traditional African art and artifacts. ○ *1½ hr. 144 W. 125th St. (btw. Lenox Ave. & Adam Clayton Powell, Jr., Blvd.). ☎ 212/864-4500. www.studiomuseum.org. Admission $7 adults, $3 seniors & students, free for children 12 & under (free admission for all Sun). Thurs–Fri noon–9pm, Sat 10am–6pm, Sun noon–6pm. Subway: 2/3/A/B/C/D to 125th St.*

7 ★★ Red Rooster Harlem. For a taste of modern Harlem, hit up chef Marcus Samuelsson's cheerful comfort food hot spot. Don't miss the signature Fried Yardbird. *310 Lenox Ave. (btw. 125th & 126th sts.). ☎ 212/792-9001. www.redroosterharlem.com. $$–$$$.*

8 National Jazz Museum in Harlem. The interim home of the National Jazz Museum offers up a small visitor center with books, CDs, and photographs, including a print of *A Great Day in Harlem.* Art Kane, a photographer for *Esquire,* took the famous black-and-white photograph of 57 assembled jazz greats—including Charles Mingus, Thelonious Monk, Lester Young, and Mary Lou Williams—on the steps of a brownstone in 1958. ○ *20 min. 104 E. 126th St. (btw. Lexington & Park aves.). ☎ 212/348-8300. www.jazzmuseuminharlem.org. Mon–Fri 10am–4pm. Subway: 4/5/6 to 125th St.*

9 Astor Row. Built by the Astor family in the 1880s, this 28-home row of red-brick town houses might remind you of a sleepy block in Savannah, Georgia, but in reality, it's just another architectural wonder of Harlem. Recently the porches of the homes were restored, and now most of the 28 residences have returned to their former glory. ○ *20 min. 130th St. (btw. Fifth & Lenox aves.). Subway: 2/3 to 135th St.*

10 ★★★ Schomburg Center for Research in Black Culture. This national research library has more than five million items documenting the experiences of African

Bustling 125th Street in Harlem.

The Mount Morris Park Historic District.

Americans. The collections include manuscripts and rare books, moving images and recorded sound, art and artifacts, and photographs and prints. ⏱ *45 min. 515 Malcolm X Blvd. (btw. 135th & 136th sts.).* ☎ *212/491-2200. www.nypl.org. Free admission. Mon–Wed noon–8pm, Thurs–Fri 11am–6pm, Sat 10am–5pm. Subway: 2/3 to 135th St.*

⑪ Abyssinian Baptist Church. This Baptist church's congregation first gathered downtown in 1808, when a group of African Americans and Ethiopians withdrew from the First Baptist Church to protest its segregated seating. The congregation grew here in 1922 under the leadership of Adam Clayton Powell, Sr. (his son was the preacher, activist, and congressman for whom the nearby boulevard was named). You can join Sunday services at 9am and 11am; the interior is open at odd hours otherwise. ⏱ *20 min. 132 W. Odell Clark Place (formerly 138th St., btw. Malcolm X Blvd. & Adam Clayton Powell, Jr., Blvd.).* ☎ *212/862-7474. www.abyssinian. org. Subway: 2/3 to 135th St.*

⑫ ★ Strivers' Row. Hardly a brick has changed among these McKim, Mead & White neo–Italian Renaissance town houses since they were built in 1890. Once the original owners had moved out, the brownstones attracted the cream of the new Harlem, including such "strivers" as Eubie Blake and W. C. Handy. *W. 139th St. (btw. Adam Clayton Powell, Jr., & Frederick Douglass blvds.).*

⑬ Hamilton Grange. A national memorial since 1962, this is the only house founding father Alexander Hamilton ever owned. The rooms and original furniture were recently restored when the house, built in 1802, moved—for the third time—to its original location on a bluff just west of St. Nicholas Avenue. Ranger-guided tours are given five times a day, and the house's spacious grounds often host special concerts and other events. ⏱ *1 hr. 414 W. 141st St. (btw. St. Nicholas & Convent aves).* ☎ *212/825-6990. www.nps.gov/hagr. Daily 9am–5pm.*

The High Line

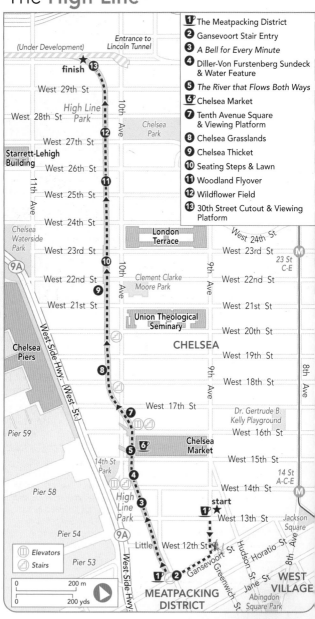

1 The Meatpacking District
2 Gansevoort Stair Entry
3 *A Bell for Every Minute*
4 Diller-Von Furstenberg Sundeck & Water Feature
5 *The River that Flows Both Ways*
6 Chelsea Market
7 Tenth Avenue Square & Viewing Platform
8 Chelsea Grasslands
9 Chelsea Thicket
10 Seating Steps & Lawn
11 Woodland Flyover
12 Wildflower Field
13 30th Street Cutout & Viewing Platform

The High Line, an abandoned West Side rail line, was smartly reinvented as an urban park a few years ago. Where freight trains once rumbled along an elevated track and weeds grew wild when the trains stopped running, now a concrete pathway winds through a landscape of naturalistic plantings and public art installations, all with Hudson River views. Combine this tour with "Chelsea's Art & Architecture" (p 70) for a leisurely day.

The High Line.

1 ★★ Breakfast in the Meatpacking District. It's the rare meatpacking truck that muscles down these cobblestoned streets anymore—the neighborhood is chockablock with bistros, boutiques, and bars. It's walkable and very pedestrian-friendly, however. Start your tour with a hearty breakfast at Pastis (9 Ninth Ave. at Little W. 12th St.; ☎ 212/929-4844; www.pastisny.com; $$$), in the heart of the neighborhood, or at the Standard Grill (848 Washington St. at 13th St.; 212/645-4100; www.thestandardgrill.com; $$$), directly beneath the High Line.

2 Gansevoort Stair Entry. The foliage in the **Gansevoort Woodland,** at the top of the stairs, changes with the seasons. In autumn, aromatic aster, smokebush, and winterberry holly dust the paths in purple and red hues. In spring, walkways are pillowed in creamy white serviceberry blossoms. The old track's rusted rails are integrated into the landscaping. *Btw. Gansevoort & Little W. 12th sts.*

3 ★★★ *A Bell for Every Minute.* From the tinkle of a child's toy phone to the joyous peal of the Trinity Church bells, a recording of a different urban bell reverberates in the covered 14th Street Passage every minute. Audio artist Stephen Vitiello created this multichannel sound installation—a deeply affecting sonic quilt of memory and a community's shared soundscape. At the top of the hour, a chorus of bells rings out. *At 14th St.*

Practical Matters

The High Line is open daily 7am to 11pm in summer (till 8pm in winter); admission is free. Dogs, bicycles, and skateboards are not allowed. It's wheelchair-accessible, with elevators at 14th, 16th, and 30th streets; has public restrooms at 16th; and is very kid-friendly. Keep in mind that the High Line's landscaping is at its loveliest in spring, summer, and fall.

❹ ★★ **Diller–Von Fursten- berg Sundeck & Water Fea- ture.** Grab yourself a wooden chaise and admire the river views. Dip your toes in the scrim of water—a flat- tened waterfall, if you will—running the length of the sundeck. The bub- bling almost drowns out the noise of the traffic. *Btw. 14th & 15th sts.*

❺ ★★★ *The River That Flows Both Ways.* On a single day in 2008, artist Spencer Finch photo- graphed the Hudson River's surface 700 times in 700 minutes, capturing the colors that resulted from the play of light and movement on the water. The result is 700 panes of colored glass (each pane based on a single isolated pixel), arranged chronologically in the steel mullions of the High Line's old loading dock. Just like the river, the colors in the panes shift in a dance of light and shadow. *Btw. 15th & 16th sts.*

❻ ★★ **Chelsea Market.** Exit at 16th Street to find this former Nabisco factory (at 75 Ninth Ave.), now an excellent food court. If it's a nice day, get your lunch to go and head back up to the High Line to the Chelsea Market plaza, with tables with river views. *See p 70.*

❼ ★ **Tenth Avenue Square & Viewing Platform.** Crowds flock to these tiered wooden bleachers plunked virtually on top of Tenth Avenue. You can stare down the traffic on Tenth through the big picture window—and the folks below can stare up. *At 17th St.*

❽ ★ **Chelsea Grasslands.** Spring sees daffodils and hundreds of pink-and-white Lady Jane tulips. By late summer, prairie grasslands bend in the breeze. Take a seat on the wooden platforms for prime viewing all around. To the east, you'll spot the needle spire of the Empire State Building. To the west (btw. 18th and 19th sts.) is Frank Gehry's fanciful IAC office building. Across Eleventh Avenue is the Chelsea Piers sports complex, with a golf driving range atop a Hudson River pier. *Btw. 17th & 19th sts.*

❾ ★ **Chelsea Thicket.** This dense planting of flowering shrubs and small trees includes hollies, winterberry, and redbud. *Btw. 20th & 21st sts.*

❿ **Seating Steps & Lawn.** Here, where extra tracks once served as loading decks for adja- cent warehouses, is a 4,900-square- foot swath of turf for sunbathing and picnicking. Stepped seating made of reclaimed teak anchors the southern end. At the northern end, a rise in the lawn lifts visitors above the walkway, with views of Brooklyn to the east and the Hud- son River to the west. *Btw. 22nd & 23rd sts.*

The Tenth Avenue Viewing Platform.

⓫ ★★ **Philip A. and Lisa Maria Falcone Flyover.** A dense grove of tall shrubs and trees once grew between the tracks here when the trains stopped running. Today, a metal walkway rises 8 feet above the High Line's path, carrying visitors through a leafy sumac-and-magnolia tree line. *Btw. 25th & 26th sts.*

⓬ ★★ **Wildflower Field.** A landscape dominated by tough drought-resistant grasses and wildflowers took root on the High Line when trains stopped running. The modern-day landscape is planted not only with a variety of blooms but many of the same native species that survived. *Btw. 26th & 29th sts.*

⓭ ★★ **30th Street Cutout & Viewing Platform.** This viewing platform allows visitors to peer down through the grid of steel beams and girders to the traffic passing below on 30th Street. *At 30th St.*

What Was the High Line?

The railroad built America's Wild West, but it also helped build downtown Manhattan, where street-level freight trains chugged along the city's gritty West Side in the mid-1800s. Alas, as street traffic increased, Tenth Avenue became known as "Death Avenue" for its glut of gruesome accidents. But it wasn't until 1929 that the city did something about the problem, creating the West Side Improvement Project, which elevated miles of railroad track above the fray. The High Line opened in 1934, running from 34th Street to Spring Street. It bustled along for another 20 or 30 years before competition from trucking put it out of business. In 1999, the preservation of the old rail line entered the collective consciousness when the Friends of the High Line was founded by two neighborhood residents. Ten years later, the first section opened to the public. For more information, go to **www.thehighline.org**.

Chelsea's Art & Architecture

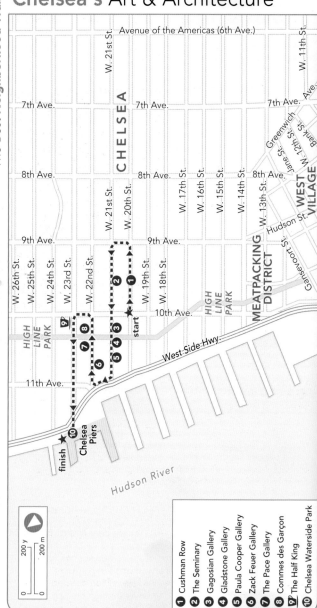

Avenue of the Americas (6th Ave.)

CHELSEA

WEST VILLAGE

MEATPACKING DISTRICT

HIGH LINE PARK

HIGH LINE PARK

West Side Hwy.

Chelsea Piers

finish

start

Hudson River

1 Cushman Row
2 The Seminary
3 Gagosian Gallery
4 Gladstone Gallery
5 Paula Cooper Gallery
6 Zack Feuer Gallery
7 The Pace Gallery
8 Commes des Garçon
9' The Half King
10 Chelsea Waterside Park

200 y
200 m

In the '80s, New York's art scene was all about SoHo and the East Village, but for a decade now, the best place to browse commercial galleries has been on the western edge of the Chelsea neighborhood. It's where you'll find the densest concentration of galleries and art-world denizens. This tour is designed to pick up where "The High Line" tour left off. (Simply walk south on Tenth Ave. from the 30th St. exit of the High Line.)

❶ ★★★ David Zwirner Gallery. Architect Annabelle Selldorf designed the gorgeous new Zwirner space, which shows artists as varied as ceramist Robert Arneson and minimalist John McCracken. *537 W. 20th St. (btw. Tenth & Eleventh aves.).* ☎ *212/517-8677. www.davidzwirner.com. Tues–Sat 10am–6pm.*

❷ ★ Cushman Row. In the late 1830s, much of Chelsea's real estate was developed by a merchant named Don Alonzo Cushman. His little empire included the handsome 1840 Greek Revival houses on West 20th Street between Ninth and Tenth avenues. The houses from no. 406 to no. 418 are better known as Cushman Row (look for the plaque at no. 412). *406–418 W. 20th St. (btw. Ninth & Tenth aves.).*

❸ ★★ General Theological Seminary. Filling up an entire city block, this historic property holds the General Theological Seminary of the Episcopal Church, the denomination's oldest seminary, founded in 1817. It's a private working seminary, but visitors can tour

The Refectory at the General Theological Seminary.

the grassy grounds (the land was donated by parishioner Clement C. Moore, author of *'Twas the Night Before Christmas*), the stunning 1888 **Chapel of the Good Shepherd,** and the vaulted **Refectory** in Hoffman Hall. Built in 1899, the Refectory dining hall has been called "one of New York's most beautiful spaces." Visitors need photo ID to enter the grounds. *440 W. 21st St. (btw. Ninth & Tenth*

Practical Matters

Most galleries in Chelsea are closed on Sundays and Mondays, have special summer hours, and close temporarily (and randomly) for exhibition changes. Call ahead to see which ones are open. Most are also free.

The Picasso and Marie-Thérèse *exhibition at the Gagosian.*

aves.). ☎ 212/243-5150. www.gts.
edu. Mon–Fri 10am–3pm.

④ ★★ Gladstone Gallery.
Gladstone's sizable roster of Ameri-
can and European artists includes
such famous names as German art-
ist Rosemarie Trockel and Keith
Haring. A second location is at 515
W. 24th St. *530 W. 21st St. (btw.
Tenth & Eleventh aves.). ☎ 212/206-
7606. www.gladstonegallery.com.
Tues–Sat 10am–6pm.*

⑤ ★ Paula Cooper Gallery.
Works by such major artists as Carl
Andre, Donald Judd, Sol Lewitt,
and Jennifer Bartlett can be found
in this loftlike space. *534 W. 21st St.*

*The futuristic entryway of the Commes
des Garçon clothing store.*

*(btw. Tenth & Eleventh aves.).
☎ 212/255-1105. www.paulacooper
gallery.com. Tues–Sat 10am–6pm.*

⑥ ★★ Zack Feuer Gallery.
Cutting-edge art and thrilling new
artists are the big draws here. *548
W. 22nd St. (btw. Tenth & Eleventh
aves.). ☎ 212/989-7700. www.zach
feuer.com. Tues–Sat 10am–6pm.*

⑦ ★★ Commes des Garçons.
This shop has no number, no signage—just look for the egg-shaped
"spaceship" entryway cut into a
red-brick facade plastered with
peeling posters and graffiti, or the
vintage sign reading HEAVENLY BODY
WORKS that hovers above the arched
doorway. Then pass through the silver aluminum tunnel into a crisp
white labyrinth full of designer Rei
Kawakubo's ultraexpensive clothing. *520 W. 22nd St. (btw. Tenth &
Eleventh aves.). ☎ 212/604-9200.*

⑧ ★★★ Gagosian Gallery.
This is a must-see. Most of Chelsea's galleries aren't large enough
to hold more than one major exhibition at a time, but the white,
high-ceilinged rooms in the Gagosian feel like a mini-museum. The
gallery pulls off major shows like
2013's acclaimed Jeff Koons's
painting and sculpture exhibition.

A Day of Play at Chelsea Piers

All this art and history got your blood going? It may be time to hit the links. Yes, at the massive Chelsea Piers sports complex, you can drive golf balls out over the Hudson River (caught by a giant net, of course) to your heart's content. The views aren't bad either. The complex also has a bowling alley, batting cages, two sundecks, an ice rink, and basketball courts. *23rd St. & Hudson River.* ☎ *212/336-6400. www.chelseapiers.com. $25 for 90 balls (peak), 147 balls (off-peak); club rentals $4. Oct–Mar daily 6:30am–11pm; Apr–Sept daily 6:30am–midnight. Bus: M23. Subway: C/E to 23rd St.*

555 W. 24th St. (btw. Tenth & Eleventh aves.). ☎ *212/741-1111. www.gagosian.com. Mon–Sat 10am–6pm.*

❾ ★ The Pace Gallery. This is one of the neighborhood's best-known galleries, so expect to see the work of major artists living and dead—from Chuck Close to Mark Rothko. Pace has another Chelsea outpost at 534 W. 25th St. *508–510 W. 25th St. (btw. Tenth & Eleventh aves.).* ☎ *212/989-4258. www.thepacegallery.com. Tues–Sat 10am–6pm.*

❿ ★ The Half King. This casual pub has a fine selection of draft and bottled beers and serves an array of burgers—from the salmon/ crab cake on a bun to the antelope burger—as well as salads, soups, and comfort dishes like mac 'n' cheese and potpie. *505 W. 23rd St. (at Tenth Ave.).* ☎ *212/462-4300. www.thehalfking.com. $–$$.*

⓫ Chelsea Waterside Park. Walk off the pub food: Next door to the Chelsea Piers sports complex, Pier 62 has been beautifully landscaped and has a California-style skatepark and a sweet little carousel with hand-carved Hudson Valley woodland creatures. Grounds curve down to the river, where you can sit and take in the glittering Hudson River panorama. *Across Eleventh Ave. at 23rd St. & West Side Hwy.*

The skatepark at Chelsea Waterside Park.

Greenwich Village

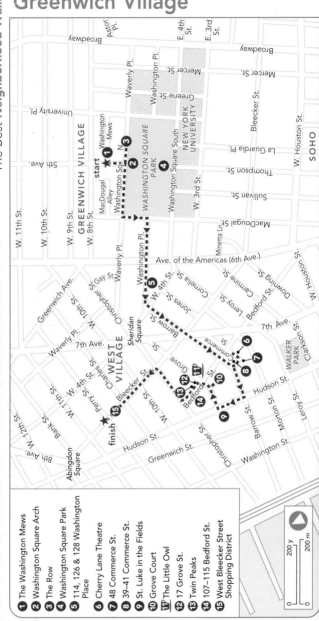

200 y
200 m

0
0

This storied neighborhood has been home to writers, painters, and entertainers for decades. It's also one of Manhattan's most picturesque and historic districts; its small scale, mazelike street plan, and dearth of skyscrapers and industrial space lend it a cozy neighborhood feel.

❶ ★ The Washington Mews.

Visitors who stumble upon this cobbled alleyway discover a living slice of old New York. The north side of the mews consists of original 19th-century stables that were converted into stuccoed houses in pale pastels—in some, the stable doors are integrated into the designs. The south side was built in 1939 to mirror the north but lacks the offbeat grace notes of the original. *Enter at University Place or Fifth Ave. (btw. 8th St. & Waverly Place).*

❷ ★ Washington Square Arch.

This impressive Roman-style arch, designed by Stanford White, was first built of wood in 1889 to commemorate the centennial of George Washington's inauguration; the current version was completed in 1891 in white marble. The arch is one of the most important landmarks in lower New York. Over the years, it has come to symbolize the neighborhood's spirit of freedom and individuality. *Fifth Ave. & Waverly Place.*

❸ ★★ The Row.

These are some of Manhattan's most celebrated town houses, built in elegant Greek Revival style in 1833 for society's blue bloods. Henry James's heroine in *Washington Square* lived here, as did many memorable characters in Edith Wharton's novels. The town houses at Washington Square North 7–13 have been gutted, with only their facades intact, but the survivors to the west at 19–26 remain more or less whole. *1–26 Washington Sq. N. (btw. Fifth Ave. & University Place).*

❹ Washington Square Park.

This relatively small park gets plenty of use (some say overuse) from local residents, New York University students, long-in-the-tooth guitarists, dog-walkers, and assorted street performers. The land on which it was built in the 1820s was once a cemetery for victims of yellow fever, and a centuries-old elm that still stands in the northwest corner of the park was the site of public hangings. These days, the roguish quality persists, but the park has undergone a thorough renovation, and it's never looked better. Centuries-old shade trees form a canopy for wide lawns and densely planted flower meadows. *Bordered by University & Waverly places and W. 4th & Macdougal sts.*

Lion sculptures guard buildings on Washington Square's Row.

⑤ 114, 126 & 128 Washington Place. Note the fancy boot scrapers on the wrought-iron stair railings from the days when transportation was largely on horseback and the streets were filled with horse manure. As you stroll, you'll spot boot scrapers of varying design all over the Village. *114 Washington Place (btw. Bedford St. & Sixth Ave.).*

⑥ Cherry Lane Theatre. Writer/poet Edna St. Vincent Millay and her artist peers converted an 1817 box factory into the Cherry Lane Playhouse in 1924. In 1929, legendary acting teacher Lee Strasberg directed F. Scott Fitzgerald's only published full-length play, *The Vegetable*, here. (It closed after 13 performances.) It's still a working theater; call to see what's playing during your visit. *38 Commerce St. (at Bedford St.).* ☎ *212/989-2020. www.cherrylanetheatre.org.*

The private entrance at Grove Court.

⑦ 48 Commerce St. Note the working gas lamp in front of the 1844 home of dry-goods merchant Alexander Stewart. The New York Gas Light Company began laying gas pipes in 1823, and gas lamps—many with ornamental post designs—continued to shine into the 20th century. *48 Commerce St. (at Barrow St.).*

⑧ ★★ 39–41 Commerce St. These three-story twin houses are among the most striking examples of early-19th-century architecture in the Village. The fact that they neatly mirror one another heightens the visual appeal. Topped with elegant mansard roofs and linked by a courtyard, nos. 39 and 41 were built in 1831 and 1832, respectively. *39 Commerce St. (at Barrow St.).*

⑨ ★ St. Luke in the Fields. This charming little church is a reconstruction of the original, which was built in 1822 and badly damaged by fire in 1981. The site on Hudson Street was donated by Trinity Church, and, from 1891 to 1976, St. Luke's was part of Trinity Parish. One of the church's founding wardens was Clement C. Moore, a gentleman scholar perhaps best known as the author of *'Twas the Night Before Christmas.* You're welcome to stroll about the interior and linger in the pretty church gardens (open Tues–Sun 8:30am–dusk). *487 Hudson St. (at Grove St.).*

⑩ ★ Grove Court. This charming gated mews set back from the street was once considered a slum; it was built for working men around 1853, when it was known as "Mixed Ale Alley." Today, the genteel Greek Revival structures share a large open courtyard—a rarity in a city where space is at a premium. *10–12 Grove St. (btw. Hudson & Bedford sts.).*

The Little Owl.

★ **The Little Owl.** The quintessential Village bistro—small, candlelit, cozy—comforts with meatball sliders and an American-Mediterranean menu. *90 Bedford St. (at Grove St.).* ☎ *212/741-4695. http://the littleowlnyc.com. $$–$$$.*

⑫ ★★ **17 Grove St.** This 1822 house is one of the last remaining wood-framed houses in the Village. Note the little 1823 cottage in back (behind the slatted fence) at 100 Bedford St. It was the workshop of the former owner, a sash maker. *17 Grove St. (at Bedford St.).*

⑬ **Twin Peaks.** This 1830 house was given a fanciful Tudor-esque renovation in 1925. It stands out among the straightforward 19th-century architecture all around it. *102 Bedford St. (at Grove St.).*

⑭ **107–115 Bedford St.** These Greek Revival town houses from the mid-1800s have boot scrapers amid the fanciful ironwork. *107 Bedford St. (at Grove St.).*

⑮ ★ **West Bleecker Street Shopping District.** West Bleecker Street, from Christopher Street to Bank Street, has become a trendy boutique alley almost overnight. Small-scale and pleasant to stroll, it's now home to **Intermix** (no. 365; ☎ 212/929-7180), **Ralph Lauren** (nos. 380–381; ☎ 212/645-5513), **Marc Jacobs** (nos. 382, 385, 400, and 403–405; ☎ 212/924-6126), **Lulu Guinness** (no. 394; ☎ 212/367-2120), and more. *W. Bleecker St. (btw. Christopher & Bank sts.).*

Boho Ghosts

Nineteenth-century writers such as Mark Twain, Edgar Allan Poe, and Henry James and painter Winslow Homer first gave the Village its reputation for embracing the unconventional. Such groundbreaking artists as Edward Hopper and Jackson Pollock were drawn in later, as were writers Eugene O'Neill, e e cummings, and Dylan Thomas. Radical thinkers from John Reed to Upton Sinclair basked in the neighborhood's liberal ethos, and in the mid–20th century, beatniks Allen Ginsberg, Jack Kerouac, and William Burroughs dug the free-swinging vibe.

Prospect Park & Park Slope

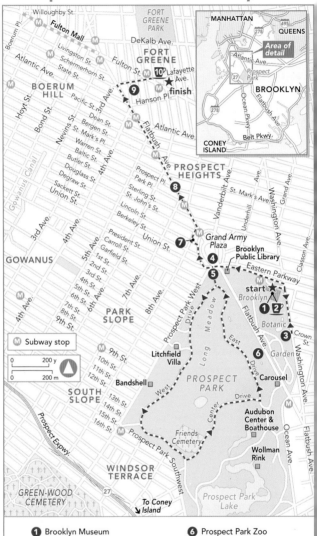

MANHATTAN

QUEENS

Area of detail

BROOKLYN

CONEY ISLAND

FORT GREENE PARK

FORT GREENE

BOERUM HILL

GOWANUS

PARK SLOPE

SOUTH SLOPE

PROSPECT HEIGHTS

PROSPECT PARK

WINDSOR TERRACE

GREEN-WOOD CEMETERY

Grand Army Plaza

Brooklyn Public Library

start

Litchfield Villa

Bandshell

Carousel

Audubon Center & Boathouse

Wollman Rink

Prospect Park Lake

To Coney Island

finish

Friends Cemetery

Ⓜ Subway stop

0 ___ 200 y
0 ___ 200 m

1 Brooklyn Museum
2 Museum Cafe
3 Brooklyn Botanic Garden
4 Grand Army Plaza
5 Prospect Park

6 Prospect Park Zoo
7 The Montauk Club
8 Flatbush Avenue
9 BAM Rose Cinemas
10 Stonehome Wine Bar

The attractions in and around Prospect Park are well worth the 25-minute subway ride from midtown Manhattan. Expect gorgeous parkland designed by Frederick Law Olmsted and Calvert Vaux (the masterminds of Central Park), the city's second-largest art museum, plus lovely 19th-century brownstones and hip clothing boutiques.

The Brooklyn Museum.

a dramatic plaza complete with fountains in 2004. ⏱ *2–3 hr. 200 Eastern Pkwy. (at Washington Ave.).* ☎ *718/638-5000. www.brooklynmuseum.org. Admission $12 adults, $8 seniors & students, free for children 12 & under. Wed 11am–6pm, Thurs 11am–10pm, Fri–Sun 11am–6pm, first Sat of every month 5–11pm. Subway: 2/3 to Eastern Pkwy.*

2 **Museum Café and Saul.** These ground-floor eateries ($–$$) helmed by acclaimed chef Saul Bolton are ideal spots to refuel before you continue. But if the weather's fine, the charms of the casual outdoor cafe ($) at the Botanic Garden (below) may outweigh even Saul's stellar menu.

1 ★★★ kids **Brooklyn Museum.** In any other city, this spectacular museum would be a star attraction, but in New York it's often overlooked because of its location outside Manhattan. The collection in New York's second-largest museum is well worth a trip though. Highlights include the **ancient Egyptian collection,** the **Asian art collection** (which specializes in both classic and contemporary works from Japan), and the **Luce Center for American Art** (an "open storage" annex holding 9,000 works, from Tiffany lamps to 19th-c. furniture by local artisans). Designed by architects McKim, Mead & White in 1897, the museum received

3 ★★★ **Brooklyn Botanic Garden.** This tranquil, elegant retreat is one of the most beautiful gardens in the city. It encompasses the **Cranford Rose Garden,** a **Children's Garden,** the **Osborne Garden** (3 acres/1.2 ha of formal gardens), the **Fragrance Garden** (designed for the visually impaired but appreciated by all), and the **Japanese Hill-and-Pond Garden.** In colder weather, you can investigate one of the world's largest collections of bonsai in the **C. V. Starr Bonsai Museum** and indoor plants (everything from cacti to orchids) in the **Steinhardt Conservatory.** If you come in April or May, seek out the lush carpet of bluebells and check the website for the timing of the

Cherry Blossom Festival. ⏱ *1–2 hr. 1000 Washington Ave. (at Eastern Pkwy.).* ☎ *718/623-7200. www.bbg. org. Admission $10 adults, $5 seniors & students, free for children 12 & under. Mar–Oct Tues–Fri 8am–6pm, Sat–Sun 10am–6pm; Nov–Feb until 4:30pm.*

❹ Grand Army Plaza. This multilane traffic circle and the tremendous **Soldiers' and Sailors' Memorial Arch** presiding over it are reminiscent of Paris's Place Charles de Gaulle and the Arc de Triomphe. The arch was built in 1892 to honor Union soldiers who died in the Civil War. *Within Plaza St. at the intersection of Flatbush Ave., Prospect Park W., Eastern Pkwy. & Vanderbilt Ave.*

❺ ★★★ kids Prospect Park. Central Park designers Frederick Law Olmstead and Calvert Vaux considered Prospect Park to be their masterpiece. The park has 562 acres (225 ha) of woodland—including Brooklyn's last remaining virgin forest—plus meadows,

Soldiers' and Sailors' Memorial Arch at Prospect Park.

bluffs, and ponds. For the best views, enter at Grand Army Plaza and walk to your right either on the park's ring road (called West Dr. here) or on the parallel pedestrian path to Meadowport Arch, and proceed to **Long Meadow.** Overlooking Long Meadow is **Litchfield Villa,** an 1857 mansion that became the headquarters for the New York parks system. Eventually West Drive turns into Center Drive, which will take you past the **Friends' Cemetery** Quaker burial ground. Center Drive leads to East Drive, which on its way back to Grand Army Plaza passes the 1906 Beaux Arts **boathouse;** the 1912 **carousel;** the **zoo;** and **Lefferts Homestead Children's Historic House Museum** (☎ 718/789-2822), a 1783 Dutch farmhouse with a museum of period furniture and exhibits. *Bounded by Prospect Park W., Parkside Ave. & Flatbush Ave.* ☎ *718/965-8951. www. prospectpark.org.*

❻ ★ kids Prospect Park Zoo. Families won't want to miss the zoo at the eastern end of the park. Children in particular take delight in encountering the animals up close, including wallabies and prairie dogs. ⏱ *1 hr. 450 Flatbush Ave.* ☎ *718/399-7339. www.prospectparkzoo.com. Admission $8 adults, $6 seniors, $5 children 3–12. Mon–Fri 10am–5pm, Sat–Sun 10am–5:30pm (fall & winter till 4:30).*

❼ ★ The Montauk Club. The northwestern side of Prospect Park is home to the upscale neighborhood of Park Slope, and its tree-lined streets are a great place to spend an afternoon. Many of the late-19th-century brownstones have been lovingly restored (walk along Montgomery Place between Eighth

Prospect Park's Boathouse.

Ave. and Prospect Park W. to see what we mean). If there were an award for most stunning building, it would go to the **Montauk Club,** which was designed in 1891 by architect Francis H. Kimball to resemble a Venetian palace. It's a private club but hosts many public events throughout the year. *25 Eighth Ave. (at Lincoln Place).* ☎ *718/638-0800.*

8 ★ Hooti Couture. Male and female clotheshorses will love this high-quality vintage clothing-and-accessory boutique. *321 Flatbush Ave. (at Seventh Ave.).* ☎ *718/857-1977. www.hooticouture.com.*

9 BAM Rose Cinemas. When this movie theater opened in the Brooklyn Academy of Music (BAM) in 1998 near Fort Green, its art-house movies brought a much-needed cultural boost to the neighborhood. And it couldn't be more accessible: You can catch the 2, 3, 4, 5, B, D, N, R, or Q subway lines back to Manhattan at the Atlantic Avenue station, a couple blocks south of BAM on Flatbush Avenue. *Peter Jay Sharp Building, 30 Lafayette Ave. (btw. Ashland Place & St. Felix St.).* ☎ *718/636-4100. www.bam.org.*

10 Stonehome Wine Bar. This is a pleasant neighborhood place to stop in for drinks or dinner before or after a show at BAM. The seasonal menu may feature butternut squash ravioli, braised Berkshire pork shank, or seared sea scallops. *87 Lafayette Ave.* ☎ *718/624-9443. www.stonehomewinebar.com. $$–$$$.*

The Montauk Club.

Chinatown & The Lower East Side

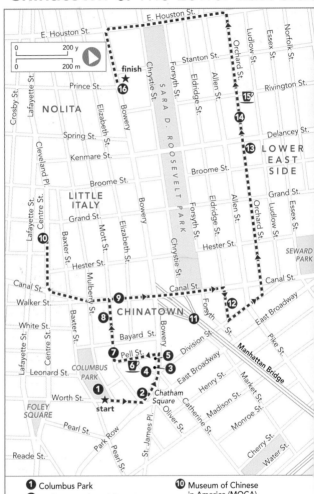

1 Columbus Park
2 Kimlau War Memorial
3 Lin Sister Herb Shop
4 Doyers Street
5 Edward Mooney House
6 Nom Wah Tea Parlor
7 Mott Street
8 Ten Ren Tea & Ginseng Co.
9 Canal Street
10 Museum of Chinese in America (MOCA)
11 Manhattan Bridge
12 Eldridge Street Synagogue
13 The Tenement Museum
14 Orchard Street
15 LES Grub
16 New Museum

L**ong known for its vibrant street life, the Lower East Side was also home to notorious slums** (including the Five Points) where Irish, Italian, Jewish, and Chinese immigrants crowded into tenements. Although much survives from that era—including many of the tenement buildings—today the neighborhood buzzes with the energy of new restaurants, bars, and live-music clubs.

❶ ★ Columbus Park. This park lies where New York's worst slum, known as Mulberry Bend, once stood, surrounded by tenements with such names as Bone Alley, Kerosene Row, and Bandits' Roost. Most of the houses were torn down in the early 20th century. The exception was the Chinatown section, which was left alone out of racist fears that the Chinese would move into other neighborhoods. *Bounded by Mosco, Mulberry, Bayard & Baxter sts.*

❷ Kimlau War Memorial. This memorial arch in Chatham Square was erected in 1962 to honor the Chinese Americans who gave their lives fighting in World War II. The square also contains an imposing statue of Lin Zexu, a 19th-century antidrug hero in China. *Chatham Sq.*

❸ ★★ Lin Sister Herb Shop. This three-story apothecary is a marvel. A wall of wooden drawers, each containing medicinal herbs, dominates the first floor. On the upper levels, reflexology massage and acupuncture treatments are offered, and a homeopathic doctor is available for consultations. *4 Bowery (at Division St.).* ☎ *212/962-5417. www.linsister.com.*

❹ Doyers Street. As you walk along Bowery, keep an eye out for Doyers Street, a narrow, crooked alleyway. This area was once notorious for activity by gangs known as tongs. The "activity" was mainly of the violent sort and often involved hatchets, which gave rise to the

An acupuncture model at the Lin Sister Herb Shop.

term "hatchet man"). Doyers Street has a sharp bend in it—locals call it an elbow—which made it impossible to see who was around the corner.

❺ ★★ Nom Wah Tea Parlor. Nom Wah has been open since 1920, making it the oldest dim sum joint in Chinatown. Formica tables, wood booths, red chairs—this oldie is definitely a goodie. Not to be missed is the egg roll, which it claims is the "original." Whether it is or not, you'll probably not find one as fresh and light elsewhere. *13 Doyers St. (btw. Bowery & Pell St.).* ☎ *212/962-6047. www.nomwah. com. $.*

Manhattan Bridge.

6 Edward Mooney House.
This Georgian brick structure, painted red, is the oldest row house in the city, dating from George Washington's New York days. Wealthy merchant Edward Mooney had the house built in 1785 on property abandoned by a Tory during the American Revolution. *18 Bowery (at Pell St.).*

7 ★ Mott Street. This is the heart of old Chinatown and the epicenter of the boisterous Chinese New Year celebrations that begin with the first full moon after January 21. But it's a great place to wander and shop any time of year. Some addresses to note: no. 17, where, down a set of steps, you will dine in grungy glory on such Chinese-American classics as sweet and sour chicken at legendary **Wop Hop; New Age Designer** at no. 38, for a traditional Chinese cheongsam made of colorful Chinese silk for around $400; and **Golden Fung Wong Bakery** at no. 41, for fresh-baked egg tarts or a big bag of fortune cookies to take home.

8 ★ Ten Ren Tea & Ginseng Co. The famous Taiwanese tea maker Ten Ren has a particularly charming outpost on Mott Street. Some of the teapots on display are museum-worthy, and the selection of teas is hard to beat. *75 Mott St. (btw. Canal & Bayard sts.).* ☎ *212/349-2286. www.tenrenusa.com.*

9 Canal Street. From West Broadway to the Manhattan Bridge, this is one of the city's liveliest and most congested thoroughfares. Stalls hawk everything from "designer" handbags to electronics. **Kam Man,** at no. 200, has a supermarket upstairs (great for candy made in Japan) and a massive collection of ceramics downstairs. Other good bets are **Pearl Paint** (p 94) and **195 Dragon Jewelry** at no. 195 for beautifully carved jade.

10 ★★ kids Museum of Chinese in America (MOCA). It is difficult to comprehend the cruel hardships that the first generations of Chinese suffered in New York. Moving into a brand-new space on Centre Street in fall 2008, this museum documents the history and culture of the Chinese in America from the early 1800s to the present. ⏱ *45 min. 215 Centre St. (btw. Howard & Grand sts.).* ☎ *212/619-4785. www.mocanyc.org. Admission $10 adults, $5 seniors & students, free for kids 12 & under; free for all Thurs. Mon & Fri 11am–5pm, Thurs 11am–9pm, Sat–Sun 10am–5pm. Subway: N/R/Q/J/Z/6 to Canal St.*

11 ★ Manhattan Bridge. This 1905 suspension bridge may not be as artistically inspired as the Brooklyn Bridge, but the monumental Beaux Arts colonnade and arch at its entrance are quite arresting. *Canal St. & Bowery.*

12 ★★ Museum at Eldridge. When this former synagogue was built by Eastern European Jews in 1887, it was the most magnificent on the Lower East Side. Its congregation once included such luminaries as Eddie Cantor, Jonas Salk, and

Ducks hanging in a Chinatown restaurant's window.

Edward G. Robinson. Over the years, however, membership declined, and the structure fell into disrepair in the 1950s. A recent $20-million renovation restored the building to its former glory—and then some. One highlight amendment to the original Herter Brothers design is a new central window by celebrated artist Kiki Smith. ⏱ *20 min. 12 Eldridge St. (btw. Canal & Division sts.).* ☎ *212/219-0302. www. eldridgestreet.org. Admission $10 adults, $8 seniors & students, $6 children 5–18, free for children 4 & under; free for all Mon. Sun–Thurs 10am–5pm, Fri 10am–3pm. Subway: B/D to Grand St. or 6/N/R to Canal St.*

⓭ ★★★ kids **The Tenement Museum.** Conceived as a monument to the experience of "urban pioneers" in America, this don't-miss museum documents the lives of immigrant residents in a six-story tenement built in 1863 at 97 Orchard St. (accessible only via the highly recommended guided tours). Among several tours to choose from, the living-history **Meet Victoria Confino tour** tells of the hardscrabble life that many immigrants faced in the late 19th and early 20th centuries. *See p 53.*

⓮ **Orchard Street.** In the 19th century, this street was a vast outdoor marketplace lined with rows of pushcarts. Today, stores have replaced the pushcarts, but in the spirit of tradition, many shop owners are willing to haggle over prices. You can also discover the stylish little boutiques and cafes that have sprung up in the neighborhood. It's a brand-new melting pot. On Sundays, the street is closed to vehicular traffic between

Museum at Eldridge Street.

Hats on display on Orchard Street.

Delancey and Houston streets. Keep in mind that many of the shops are closed Friday afternoon and Saturday for the Jewish Sabbath. Stop in at the **Lower East Side Visitor Center** at 54 Orchard St. (☎ 212/226-9010; www. lowereastsideny.com) for maps and more information. Then wander Orchard Street between Rivington and Grand streets and check out the array of stores, both old and new. You'll come across such old-timers as **Zarin Fabrics** (314 Grand; ☎ 212/925-6112; www.zarinfabrics. com), which offers beautiful fabrics and trims; and **Altman Luggage** (135 Orchard St.; ☎ 212/254-7275), which has been selling quality luggage at good prices since 1920.

15 LES Eats. Meat eaters should make a beeline for the Dagwood-style pastrami sandwiches at Katz's Delicatessen (p 120). For a taste of the old world, head to Kossar's Bialys (367 Grand St., btw. Essex & Norfolk sts; ☎ 212/473-4810; $). Maybe the best pancakes in the city can be had at the Clinton St. Baking

Company (4 Clinton St., btw. Houston & Stanton sts; ☎ 646/602/6263). If there is such a thing as New York gelato, you'll find it at Il Labotorio del Gelato (188 Ludlow St., at Houston St., ☎ 212/343-9922), where the flavors range from chestnut honey to wasabi.

16 New Museum. This 30-year-old collection of contemporary art now resides in an off-kilter stack of aluminum mesh cubes, designed by Kazuyo Sejima and Ryue Nishizawa, teetering over the Bowery's brick tenement buildings. Don't miss the view of the neighborhood from the seventh-floor observation deck, open to the public on weekends. ⏱ *1½ hr. 235 Bowery (at Prince btw. Stanton and Rivington sts.). ☎ 212/219-1222. www.newmuseum.org. Admission $14 adults, $12 seniors, $10 students, free for children 18 & under; free for all Thurs 7–9pm. Wed & Fri–Sun 11am–6pm, Thurs 11am–9pm. Subway: 6 to Spring St.; N/R to Prince St.* ●

Shopping **Best Bets**

Best **Food "Store"**
Union Square Greenmarket (p 99)

Best **Place to Deck Out Your Dream House**
ABC Carpet & Home, 881 & 888 Broadway (p 100)

Best **Footwear**
Jeffrey New York, 449 W. 14th St. (p 97)

Best **All-Around Department Store**
Bloomingdale's, 1000 Third Ave. (p 95)

Best **Browsing**
MoMA Store, 44 W. 53rd St. (p 100); and Pearl River, 477 Broadway (p 94)

Best **Toy Store**
Playing Mantis, 32 N. Moore St. (p 102)

Best **Men's Designer Clothes**
Bergdorf Goodman for Men, 754 Fifth Ave. (p 95)

Best **Women's Designer Clothes**
Bergdorf Goodman, 754 Fifth Ave. (p 95)

Best **Clothing Boutiques**
Kisan Concept Store, 125 Greene St. (p 97); and Opening Ceremony, 35 Howard St. (p 97)

Best **Cheap & Trendy Clothes**
Topshop, 478 Broadway (p 97); and UNIQLO, 546 Broadway (p 97)

Best **Vintage Jewelry**
Pippin, 72 Orchard St. (p 101)

Best **Wine & Liquor**
Astor Wines, 399 Lafayette St. (p 98)

Best **Deals on Electronics**
J&R Music & Computer World, 23 Park Row (p 96)

Best **Art Supplies**
Pearl Paint, 308 Canal St. (p 94)

Best **Beauty Products**
C. O. Bigelow, 414 Sixth Ave. (p 94)

Sales-Tax Lowdown

The sales tax in New York City is 8.875 percent (4.5 percent for city sales tax, 4 percent for New York State tax, plus an additional surcharge). **No sales tax at all is charged for clothing and footwear purchases under $110.** If you have an item shipped, be sure to get proper documentation of the sale and keep the receipts handy until the merchandise arrives at your door.

Previous page: A moosehead ceramic at MacKenzie-Childs.

Downtown Shopping

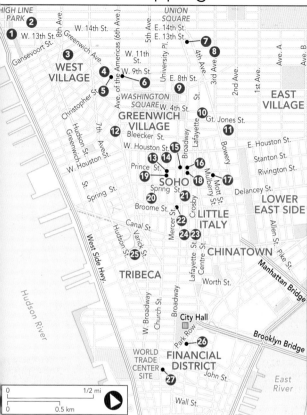

Midtown & Uptown Shopping

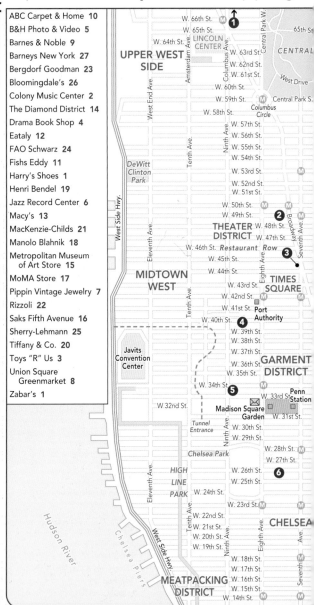

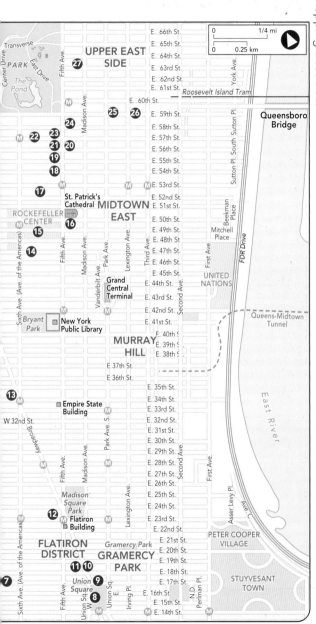

Shopping A to Z

Art Supplies

★ **Pearl Paint** CHINATOWN All the cool art students shop at this Canal Street institution. It's hands-down New York's best discount art-supply store. *308 Canal St. (btw. Broadway & Mercer sts.).* ☎ *212/431-7932. www.pearlpaint.com. AE, DISC, MC, V. Subway: N/R to Canal St.*

Beauty/Apothecary

★★ **C. O. Bigelow** GREENWICH VILLAGE Its motto—"If you can't get it anywhere else, try Bigelow's"—is right on the money. This 162-year-old apothecary carries the brands you can't find anywhere, plus its own excellent house label of personal-care products. *414 Sixth Ave. (btw. 8th & 9th sts.).* ☎ *212/533-2700. www.bigelow chemists.com. AE, DISC, MC, V. Subway: A/C/E/F/M to W. 4th St.*

★ **Kiehl's** EAST VILLAGE This 150-year-old firm's skin- and hair-care products have a cult following among the fashion crowd, and the store's free product samples add to its quirky charm. Formerly

C. O. Bigelow.

family-run, Kiehl's has been owned by L'Oréal since 2000. *109 Third Ave. (btw. 13th & 14th sts.).* ☎ *212/677-3171. www.kiehls.com. AE, DC, MC, V. Subway: 4/5/6 to Union Sq.*

★ **Space NK** SOHO This British-based shop has culled the best of the best product lines and put them all in a soothing environment. It has an added location on the Upper East Side as well as spaces in Bloomingdale's (p 95). *99 Greene St. (btw. Prince & Spring sts.).* ☎ *212/941-4200. www.spacenk.com. AE, DISC, MC, V. Subway: N/R to Prince St. or 6 to Spring St.*

Books

★★ **Barnes & Noble Union Square** UNION SQUARE This red-brick, terra-cotta relic from 1881 holds one of the chain's most impressive Manhattan stores. *Century* magazine was published here before the turn of the 20th century. *33 E. 17th St. (btw. Broadway & Park Ave.).* ☎ *212/253-0810. www.bn.com. AE, DC, DISC, MC, V. Subway: 4/5/6 to Union Sq.*

★ **Drama Book Shop** THEATER DISTRICT The play's the thing, and this little performing-arts book-store sells thousands of plays, from Greek tragedies to this year's hits. *250 W. 40th St. (btw. Eighth & Ninth aves.).* ☎ *212/944-0595. www.dramabookshop.com. AE, MC, V. Subway: A/C/E to 42nd St.*

★★ **Rizzoli** MIDTOWN WEST This gorgeous bookstore is an atmospheric place to browse for high-end visual art and design books, plus quality fiction and gourmet cookbooks. *31 W. 57th St. (btw. Fifth & Sixth aves.).* ☎ *212/759-2424. www.rizzoliusa.com. AE, MC, V. Subway: N/R to Fifth Ave.*

Barneys' chic-modern window display.

★★ The Strand UNION SQUARE This local legend is worth a visit for the staggering "18 miles of books," new and used titles at up to 85 percent off list price. *828 Broadway (at 12th St.).* ☎ *212/473-1452. www.strandbooks.com. AE, DC, DISC, MC, V. Subway: L/N/R/4/5/6 to Union Sq.*

★★ Three Lives & Co. GREENWICH VILLAGE This cozy, independent store has good stock and a knowledgeable staff. *154 W. 10th St. (near Seventh Ave.).* ☎ *212/741-2069. www.threelives.com. AE, DC, MC, V. Subway: 1 to Christopher St.*

Department Stores
★ Barneys New York MIDTOWN EAST This smart-looking store is always on the cutting edge of fashion; check out Barneys Co-op (with locations in SoHo and Brooklyn and on the Upper West Side) for less-pricey designers and solid house brands. *660 Madison Ave. (at 61st St.).* ☎ *212/826-8900. www.barneys.com. AE, MC, V. Subway: N/R to Fifth Ave.*

★★ Bergdorf Goodman MIDTOWN The place for ladies who lunch and anyone who reveres fashion and clothes built to last. It's

pricey, but the sales are terrific. The **men's store** across the street (745 Fifth Ave.) has a great selection. *754 Fifth Ave. (at 58th St.).* ☎ *800/558-1855. www.bergdorfgoodman.com. AE, DC, MC, V. Subway: E/F to Fifth Ave.*

★★ Bloomingdale's MIDTOWN EAST Packed to the gills with goods, Bloomie's is more accessible and affordable than Barneys, Bergdorf, or Saks. There's a SoHo outpost too, at 504 Broadway. *1000 Third Ave. (Lexington Ave. at 59th St.).* ☎ *212/705-2000. www.bloomingdales.com. AE, MC, V. Subway: 4/5/6 to 59th St.*

★ Henri Bendel MIDTOWN Set inside a gorgeous landmark building, this is the place for grownup girls who love the funky and the frilly. The makeup section is one of the best in the city. *712 Fifth Ave. (btw. 55th & 56th sts.).* ☎ *212/247-1100. www.henribendel.com. AE, DC, DISC, MC, V. Subway: N/R to Fifth Ave.*

Macy's HERALD SQUARE The size is unmanageable and the service is clueless, but they do sell *everything.* And *everything* goes on sale. This is where to come to get a seriously stylish—and seriously marked-down—winter coat in the January sales. *151 W. 34th St. (at Broadway).* ☎ *212/695-4400. www. macys.com. AE, MC, V. Subway: B/D/F/N/Q/R/1/2/3/ to 34th St.*

★ Saks Fifth Avenue MIDTOWN
This legendary flagship store is a classic. It stocks big-name designers in fashion, accessories, and cosmetics, all with price tags to match. Look for smartly priced house brands on the fourth and fifth floors. *611 Fifth Ave. (btw. 49th & 50th sts.).* ☎ *212/753-4000. www.saksfifth avenue.com. AE, DC, DISC, MC, V. Subway: B/D/F/Q to 47th–50th sts./ Rockefeller Center; E/F to Fifth Ave.*

Electronics
★ B&H Photo & Video GARMENT DISTRICT
This camera superstore has everything from lenses to darkroom equipment. **Note:** It's closed on Saturdays. *420 Ninth Ave. (at 34th St.).* ☎ *800/606-6969. www. bhphotovideo.com. AE, DISC, MC, V. Subway: A/C/E to 34th St.*

★ J&R Music & Computer World FINANCIAL DISTRICT
This is the city's top computer, electronics, small appliance, and office equipment retailer. *1 Park Row (at Ann St., opposite City Hall Park).* ☎ *800/806-1115 or 212/238-9000.*

Discounts on everything at Century 21.

The Prada store in SoHo.

www.jr.com. AE, DISC, MC, V. Subway: 2/3 to Park Place; 4/5/6 to Brooklyn Bridge/City Hall.

Fashion
★ Anthropologie SOHO
This chain sells funky, slightly exotic, and affordable women's clothing and accessories—not to mention original and very stylish housewares and gifts at good prices. *375 W. Broadway (btw. Spring & Broome sts.).* ☎ *212/343-7070. www.anthro pologie.com. AE, MC, V. Subway: C/E to Spring St.*

★ Century 21 FINANCIAL DISTRICT
It's easy to become addicted to the seriously discounted designer clothes here, but don't expect to be pampered or bathed in flattering

lighting. And avoid around noontime, when lunchtime working stiffs crowd the aisles in pursuit of men's, women's, and children's clothing. *22 Cortlandt St. (btw. Broadway & Church St.). ☎ 212/227-9092. www.c21stores. com. AE, MC, V. Subway: 1/2/3/4/5/M to Fulton St.; A/C to Broadway/Nassau St.; E to Chambers St.*

★★ Jeffrey New York MEAT-PACKING DISTRICT
This outpost of the famed Atlanta megaboutique may be pricey as all get out, but the staff is warm and friendly. The fantastic shoe selection makes it a worthy schlep for style hounds. *449 W. 14th St. (at 10th Ave.). ☎ 212/206-1272. www.jeffreynewyork.com. AE, MC, V. Subway: A/C/E/L to 14th St.*

★★ Kisan Concept Store
SOHO   Arriving from Paris by way of Iceland, this shop sells not only "high-street" European-branded women's wear but art books, shoes, a sprinkling of men's items, and a breathtaking selection of fine kids' clothes. *125 Greene St. (btw. Prince & Houston sts.). ☎ 212/475-2470. www.kisanstore.com. AE, MC, V. Subway: R/W to Prince St.*

★★ Opening Ceremony CHI-NATOWN/SOHO
For many the top clothing boutique in the city, Opening Ceremony has fun, cutting-edge designs from all over the world, plus a house line that is smart, good-looking, and eminently wearable. It also has a location in the Ace Hotel. *35 Howard St. (near Broadway). ☎ 212/219-2688. www.openingceremony.us. AE, MC, V. Subway: N/R/6 to Canal St.*

★ Prada SOHO
The sleek, chic Italian trendsetter occupies a spectacular space designed by architect Rem Koolhaas. *575 Broadway (at Prince St.). ☎ 212/334-8888. AE, DISC, MC, V. Subway: N/R to Prince St.*

★ Scoop MEATPACKING DISTRICT
Ever wonder what a fashion editor's closet looks like? Probably like this small women's clothing chain—a collection of pieces from a variety of designers whose work is fashion forward but not so cutting edge as to be unwearable *430 W. 14th St. (at Washington St.). ☎ 212/929-1244. www.scoopnyc.com. AE, DC, DISC, MC, V. Subway: A/C/E to 14th St.*

★ Topshop SOHO
Your teenagers may drag you to this British megastore, but don't despair: Shopping at Topshop is delicious fun. Yes, the rock-star element is here, from fringed suede to Edwardian puffy shirts, but so are wearable separates like smartly tailored boyfriend jackets and on-trend variations on the little black dress. And the stuff is priced to move! *478 Broadway (near Spring St.). ☎ 212/966-9555. www.topshop.com. AE, DISC, MC, V. Subway: 6 to Spring St.; N/R to Canal St.*

★ UNIQLO SOHO
The city's original UNIQLO location (there are also outposts on 34th and 53rd sts.) is always packed with savvy shoppers. Known as Japan's answer to the Gap, UNIQLO specializes in smartly constructed, wearable separates—like the perfect black cotton

Heaven for neat freaks: UNIQLO.

Union Square Greenmarket.

V-neck shirt for $16. *546 Broadway (at Prince St.).* ☎ *917/237-8800. AE, DC, DISC, MC, V. Subway: N/R to Prince St.; 6 to Spring St.*

Food & Wine
★★ Astor Wines & Spirits.
EAST VILLAGE With a deep stock and great values, this spacious downtown institution not only

Eataly's La Piazza wine bar.

features hard-to-find wines but has a vast collection of varied spirits at world-beating prices. *399 Lafayette St. (at E.4th St.).* ☎ *212/674-7500. www.astorwines.com. Subway: B/D/ F/M to Broadway-Lafayette St.*

★★ Dean & DeLuca SOHO
This place has everything—from excellent cheese, meat, fish, and dessert counters to fresh sushi and luscious prepared foods. *560 Broadway (at Prince St.).* ☎ *212/226-6800. www.dean-deluca.com. AE, DISC, MC, V. Subway: N/R to Prince St.*

★★ Eataly FLATIRON DISTRICT
You can dine in at this dynamic Italian-centric marketplace or shop to your heart's content. Take home armloads of good Italian pastas, olive oils and vinegars, fresh mozzarella, pastries, coffee, books, wine, and beer. *200 Fifth Ave. (at 23rd St.).* ☎ *212/229-2560. www.eataly ny.com. AE, MC, V. Market daily 10am–11pm. Restaurants daily lunch & dinner. Subway: N/R/6 to 23rd St.*

Sherry-Lehmann UPPER EAST
SIDE One of the city's best selections of wine is complemented by a savvy staff. *505 Park Ave. (btw. 59th*

& 60th sts.). ☎ 212/838-7500. www.
sherry-lehmann.com. AE, MC, V. Subway: N/R to Lexington Ave.; 4/5/6 to
59th St.

**★★ Union Square Greenmar-
ket** UNION SQUARE   At Manhattan's largest farmer's market, you'll
find fresh produce from upstate
and New Jersey farms, fish just off
the boat from Long Island, artisanal
cheeses and home-cured meats,
plants, and organic herbs and
spices. I've seen celebrated chefs
arrive here with wheelbarrows in
tow. Open year-round Mondays,
Wednesdays, Fridays, and Saturdays during daylight hours. *In Union
Sq.* ☎ 212/788-7476. www.grownyc.
org. No credit cards. Subway:
4/5/6/N/Q/R/W to Union Sq.

★★ Zabar's UPPER WEST
SIDE   The one-and-only Zabar's is
the place to go for great smoked
salmon and all the works—not to
mention terrific prepared foods,
gourmet edibles, coffees, cheeses,
you name it. *2245 Broadway (at 80th
St.).* ☎ 212/496-1234. www.zabars.
com. AE, DC, MC, V. Subway: 1 to
79th St.

Shabby chic at MacKenzie-Childs.

Gifts
★★ John Derian Company
EAST VILLAGE   Fabulous decoup-
age items, colorful candleholders
handmade in Paris, and terra-cotta
pottery are but a few of the delicious treats here. *6 E. 2nd St. (btw.
Second Ave. & the Bowery).*
☎ 212/677-3917. www.johnderian.
com. AE, MC, V. Subway: 6 to
Bleecker St., F/M to Second Ave.

★★ Le Fanion GREENWICH
VILLAGE   Beautiful French Country
pottery in a charming Village shop.
299 W. 4th St. (at Bank St.). ☎ 212/
463-8760. www.lefanion.com. AE,
MC, V. Subway: 1//2/3 at 14th St.

★ MacKenzie-Childs MIDTOWN
Whimsy in a teacup. Colorful, artisanal dinnerware, hand-painted furniture, and home furnishings in a
delightful store. *20 W. 57th St. (btw.
Fifth & Sixth aves.).* ☎ 212/570-
6050. www.mackenzie-childs.com.
AE, MC, V. Subway: N/R to Fifth Ave.

**★★ Metropolitan Museum of
Art Store** MIDTOWN   Great for
jewelry, china, books, toys, textiles,
umbrellas, and objets d'art

ABC Carpet & Home.

modeled on the Met's collection. See the website for other branch locations. *15 W. 49th St. (at Rockefeller Center).* ☎ *212/332-1360. www.metmuseum.org/store. AE, DISC, MC, V. Subway: B/D/F/M to 47th–50th sts./Rockefeller Center.*

★★★ MoMA Store

MIDTOWN   The Museum of Modern Art store stocks fabulous, unique gifts, from silk scarves with Frank Lloyd Wright designs to Eames chairs. The Christmas ornaments are gorgeous. See website for other branch locations. *44 W. 53rd St. (btw. Fifth & Sixth aves.).* ☎ *212/767-1050. www.momastore. org. AE, DISC, MC, V. Subway: E/M to Fifth Ave./53rd St.*

★★ Pearl River

SOHO   I love browsing this store, stocked with Asian clothing, housewares, foods, and gifts. *477 Broadway (Grand St.).* ☎ *212/431-4770. www.pearlriver. com. AE, DISC, MC, V. Subway: N/R to Canal St.*

Home Design & Housewares
★★★ ABC Carpet & Home

FLATIRON DISTRICT   This magical (and pricey) two-building emporium is legendary, and it deserves to be: It's the ultimate home fashions and furnishings store, with everything from zillion-thread-count sheets to enchanting children's furniture. *881 & 888 Broadway (at 19th St.).* ☎ *212/473-3000. www.abchome. com. AE, DISC, MC, V. Subway: L/N/R/4/5/6 to 14th St./Union Sq.*

★ Broadway Panhandler

GREENWICH VILLAGE   Cooks will love browsing for professional-quality cookware in this longtime favorite. *65 E. 8th St. (btw. Broadway & University Place).* ☎ *866/266-5927. www.broadwaypanhandler.com. AE, MC, V. Subway: N/R to 8th St.*

Fishs Eddy FLATIRON DISTRICT Come here for vintage and reproduction dishes, flatware, and glasses. *889 Broadway (at 19th St.).* ☎ *212/420-9020. www.fishseddy. com. AE, MC, V. Subway: L/N/R/4/5/6 to 14th St./Union Sq.*

Jewelry & Precious Stones
The Diamond District

MIDTOWN   This is the heart of the city's diamond trade, although many of the merchants deal in semiprecious stones, too. If you know your four C's, it's a great place to get a deal on diamonds; if you don't, stick with window-shopping. Most shops are open Monday to Friday only. *47th St. (btw. Fifth & Sixth aves.). Subway: B/D/F/M to Rockefeller Center.*

★ Fragments

SOHO   Looking for original pieces? Fragments sells jewelry by more than 100 artists working in various media. Prices vary dramatically, starting at $50 and spiking above $20,000. *116 Prince St. (btw. Greene & Wooster sts.).* ☎ *212/334-9588. www. fragments.com. AE, DC, DISC, MC, V. Subway: C/E to Spring St.*

★ Pippin Vintage Jewelry
CHELSEA From stately pearls to funky Bakelite, this gem of a shop carries it all. Also check out Pippin Home, a small shop selling antiques and home furnishings, behind the jewelry store. *112 W. 17th St. (btw. Sixth & Seventh aves.).* ☎ *212/505-5159. www.pippin vintage.com. AE, MC, V. Subway: A/E to 14th St.*

★★ Tiffany & Co. MIDTOWN
Deservedly famous, this iconic multilevel store carries jewelry, watches, tableware, and stemware, and a variety of gift items. Love the silver yo-yo! *727 Fifth Ave. (at 57th St.).* ☎ *212/755-8000. www.tiffany. com. AE, DC, DISC, MC, V. Subway: N/R to Fifth Ave.*

Music
★ Bleecker Street Records
GREENWICH VILLAGE The well-organized CD and LP collections include rock, jazz, folk, blues, and punk. *239 Bleecker St. (at Carmine St.).* ☎ *212/255-7899. AE, MC, V. Subway: A/C/E/F/M to W. 4th St.*

★ Jazz Record Center CHELSEA
This is the place to find rare and out-of-print jazz records. *236 W. 26th St., Room 804 (btw. Seventh & Eighth aves.).* ☎ *212/675-4480. www.jazzrecordcenter.com. AE, MC, V. Subway: 1 to 28th St.*

Perfumes/Scents
★★ Aedes De Venustas
GREENWICH VILLAGE Evoking a romantic boudoir out of the Victorian era, this whimsical spot offers exotic and hard-to-find scents. *9 Christopher St. (at Gay St.).* ☎ *212/ 206-8674. www.aedes.com. AE, MC, V. Subway: 1 to Christopher St.*

Shoes
★ Harry's Shoes UPPER WEST SIDE
This old-school shoe store doesn't sell sex (à la Manolo); it sells shoes. Great selection of comfortable styles. **Harry's Shoes for Kids** is a half-block away at 2315 Broadway. *2299 Broadway (at 83rd St.).* ☎ *866/442-7797. www.harrys-shoes.com. AE, DISC, MC, V. Subway: 1 to 79th St. or 86th St.*

Fishs Eddy's New York–centric designs.

A dinosaur at Toys "R" Us in Times Square.

★★ **Manolo Blahnik** MIDTOWN These wildly sexy women's shoes could turn anyone into a foot fetishist. *31 W. 54th St. (btw. Fifth & Sixth aves.).* ☎ *212/582-3007. AE, MC, V. Subway: E/F to Fifth Ave.*

★ **Sigerson Morrison** NOLITA Very modern shoes with clever retro detailing. *28 Prince St. (btw. Mott & Elizabeth sts.).* ☎ *212/219-3893. www.sigersonmorrison.com. AE, MC, V. Subway: B/D/F/Q to Broadway/Lafayette St.; N/R to Prince St.; 6 to Spring St.*

Toys
★★ kids **FAO Schwarz** MIDTOWN It gets crowded during the holidays, and the music can drive you nuts. But it's the mother lode of toys in New York—and the store-within-a-store toy boutiques are

adorable. *767 Fifth Ave. (at 59th St.).* ☎ *212/644-9400. www.fao.com. Subway: N/R/W to Fifth Ave. & 59th St.*

★★ kids **Playing Mantis** TRIBECA It sells "toys for life," beautiful creations crafted from natural materials: wood-carved forest-fairy houses, hand-hewn musical instruments, and other remarkable finds. *32 N. Moore St. (btw. Hudson & Varick sts.).* ☎ *646/484-6845. www.friendlymantis.com. Subway: 1 to Franklin St.*

kids **Toys "R" Us** TIMES SQUARE Check out the T-Rex on the second floor and take a spin on the Ferris wheel, if you can tear your kids away from the lavish toy displays. *1514 Broadway (at 44th St.).* ☎ *646/366-8800. AE, DISC, MC, V. Subway: 1/2/3/7//A/C/E/N/ Q/R/S to 42nd St.* ●

Central Park

1. Harlem Meer
2. Conservatory Garden
3. The Reservoir
4. The Obelisk
5. The Great Lawn
6. The Ramble
7. The Lake
8. The Loeb Boathouse
9. Bethesda Terrace
10. The Mall
11. The Carousel
12. Wollman Rink
13. Delacorte Clock
14. The Arsenal
15. Central Park Zoo

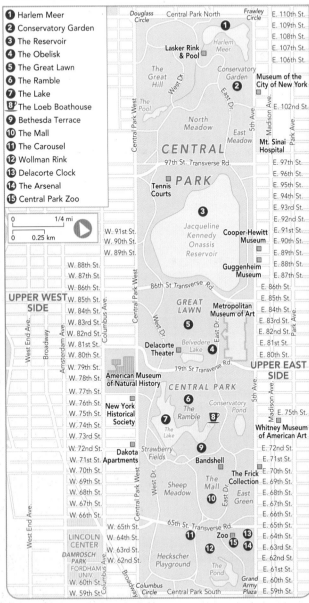

Previous page: Central Park's Bethesda Fountain.

Often called Manhattan's backyard, Central Park is all that and far more. It's a vibrant 843-acre (337-ha) masterpiece that was carved from a muddy swamp and squatters' camp in the 1850s by landscape architects Frederick Law Olmstead and Calvert Vaux. Today, thousands of residents and visitors alike flock here to stroll, run, bike, row boats, picnic, and play.

1 Harlem Meer. This 11-acre (4.4-ha) *meer* (the Dutch word for lake) wasn't part of the original Central Park. Added in 1863, it has a natural, rugged shoreline and a community of swans. The **Charles A. Dana Discovery Center** (☎ 212/860-1370), on the northern shore, contains a year-round visitor center and hosts Central Park Conservancy seasonal exhibitions, community programs, and holiday celebrations in its Great Hall. *Fifth Ave. from 106th–110th sts.*

2 ★★ Conservatory Garden. This formal garden was commissioned by the WPA (Work Projects Administration) in 1936. Its showpieces are many: an elegant Italian garden built around a classical fountain, a mazelike English garden, a bronze statue of the children from the novel *The Secret Garden* standing in a reflecting pool. In summer, water lilies float in the pool, and flowering plants and shrubs fill the garden. To reach the Reservoir (see below) from here, walk south through the park or, to save a mile of walking, take any bus down Fifth Avenue and get off at 86th Street. *Fifth Ave. & 105th St.*

3 The Reservoir. Created in 1862 as part of the Croton Water System, the Reservoir was in use until 1994. Occupying 106 acres (42 ha) and extending the width of the park, it is surrounded by bridle and running paths. Many a celebrity (Jackie O, Madonna) and civilian have jogged along the 1.6-mile (2.6km) upper track, which overlooks the reservoir and affords great skyline views. The reservoir holds a billion gallons of water and is 40 feet (12m) at its greatest depth, but these days it is only used as an emergency backup water supply. Walk along the path behind the Metropolitan Museum of Art to reach the Obelisk. *Midpark from 85th–96th sts.*

4 ★★ The Obelisk. This 71-foot (21m) artifact from Ancient Egypt was an 1881 gift to the U.S. from the khedive of Egypt. *See p 12.*

5 ★ The Great Lawn. Expansive enough for simultaneous games of softball, volleyball, or soccer, the Great Lawn is also a plum spot for a picnic—especially on those warm summer nights when the New York Philharmonic or Metropolitan Opera performs for free (p 146). Find the schedule at **www.centralparknyc.org** or **http://nyphil.org**, and bring along picnic fare from nearby gourmet groceries

Tulips blooming in the park.

Strolling alongside the Lake.

Zabar's (Broadway and 80th St.) or **Fairway** (Broadway and 75th St.). At the southern end, ★ **Belvedere Castle** (p 12) and its surrounding duck pond are particularly picturesque. *Midpark from 79th–85th sts.*

6 ★ **The Ramble.** It looks wild—especially in comparison with the rest of the park—but it was actually designed that way to mirror untamed nature. Olmstead called it his "wild garden," and it takes up 38 acres (15 ha) of the park. The Ramble has a seedy reputation after dark (I might not set foot in it after sunset), but during the day it's wonderful to explore. The curving paths that lead through the wooded area are inviting and offer some of the best scouting ground for bird-watchers in the city—some 230 species have been spotted here so far. A statue of a crouching cougar overlooks the East Drive between 76th and 77th streets. *Midpark from 73rd–79th sts.*

7 ★★ **The Lake.** It's not quite as large as the Reservoir, but it's by far the most beautiful body of water in the park. Who would guess this idyllic lake was once a swamp? Rent a rowboat or kayak ($12 for the first hour) at the Loeb

Boathouse (see below) and take your sweetie for a turn around the lake—the views from the water are superb. *Midpark from 71st–78th sts.*

8 ★ **The Loeb Boathouse.** At the eastern end of the Lake is the Loeb Boathouse, where you can rent boats and bikes as well as dine—and dine well. The upscale Lakeside Restaurant (lunch/brunch year-round; dinner Apr–Nov) is a truly lovely fine-dining space with alfresco lakeside seating on a wooden deck under a white canopy. The menu is contemporary American. The casual Boathouse Bar & Grill is popular in the warm months (Apr–Nov 11am–11pm daily) and the Express Café serves breakfast and light fare (year-round 8am–8pm daily). *Fifth Ave. (btw. 74th & 75th sts.).* ☎ *212/517-2233. www.thecentralparkboathouse.com. $–$$$.*

9 ★★ **Bethesda Terrace.** Architects Olmstead and Vaux were both determined to put nature first, second, and third (as Vaux was once quoted saying), but they acknowledged the need for a central meeting place in Central Park. This two-tiered terrace as well as *Bethesda, the Angel of the Waters,* the sculpture at its center, were part of the original design. *Midpark at 72nd St.*

10 ★★ **The Mall.** This beguiling promenade is shaded by a curving canopy of American elms—a favorite tree of the park's designers. At the south end of the Mall is the **Literary Walk,** flanked by statues of Shakespeare, Robert Burns, Sir Walter Scott, and other historic and literary figures. *Midpark from 66th–72nd sts.*

⑪ **kids The Carousel.** It's hard to believe that this beautiful vintage carousel was ever relegated to a dusty warehouse. The original carousel was built in 1871; fires destroyed it and a successor. Park officials searched high and low for a replacement, only to discover this treasure abandoned in an old trolley building on Coney Island. The 58 colorful steeds on it are among the largest carousel ponies in the world and were hand-carved by Russian immigrants Solomon Stein and Harry Goldstein in 1908. *Mid-park at 64th St.* ☎ *212/439-6900, ext. 12. $3 ride. Apr–Oct daily 10am–6pm; Nov–Mar call.*

⑫ **kids Trump (Wollman) Rink and Victorian Gardens Amusement Park.** Formerly known and forever remembered as Wollman Rink, this wintertime park treasure was first set up in 1951. In summer, the spot is home to the immaculate Victorian Gardens Amusement Park, geared toward young children. *Fifth Ave. (btw. 62nd & 63rd sts.). Trump Rink:* ☎ *212/439-6900. www.wollmanskatingrink.com. Mon–Tues 10am–2:30pm, Wed–Thurs 10am–10pm, Fri–Sat 10am–11pm, Sun 10am–9pm. Admission $11–$17 adults, $6–$9 children 11 & under; skate rental $7. Victorian Gardens:* ☎ *212/982-2229. www.victorian gardensnyc.com. Daily 11am–7pm. Admission w/ unlimited rides $21.*

⑬ **The Arsenal.** This Gothic Revival building actually predates the park. It looks like a fortress—which it briefly was when it housed troops during the Civil War. It later served as the original home of the American Museum of Natural History (p 54). It was even home to some of P. T. Barnum's circus animals, from a black bear to white swans. Today, it houses the park headquarters and a third-floor art gallery. *Fifth Ave. & 64th St.* ☎ *311 in New York City or 212/NEW-YORK.*

⑭ ★★ **kids Central Park Zoo.** The Central Park Zoo was built in 1988 to replace a 1934 WPA-built structure that had become cramped and outdated. Today the zoo's 5½ acres (2.2 ha) house more than 400 animals. Watch the sea lions cavorting in the Central Garden pool, the polar bears splashing around in their watery den, or the penguins being fed in the chilly Polar Circle. In the small **Tisch Children's Zoo,** kids can feed and pet tame farm animals, including pot-bellied pigs. Don't miss the **Delacorte Clock,** a timepiece with six clockwork bronze animals designed by Italian sculptor Andrea Spadini; it has been captivating park visitors since the '60s. The tunes played on the hour are longer and more elaborate; the half-hour ones are short but still sweet. ⏱ *75 min. Fifth Ave. (btw. 63rd & 66th sts.).* ☎ *212/861-6030. www.centralparkzoo.com. Admission $18 adults, $15 seniors, $13 children 3–12, free for kids 2 & under. Daily 10am–4:30pm (extended hours for weekends, holidays & spring/summer).*

A seal preening at the Central Park Zoo.

Green-Wood Cemetery

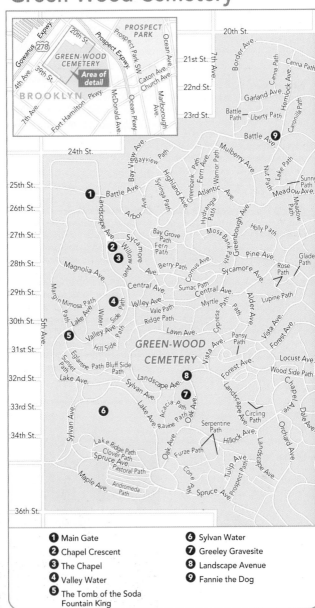

1 Main Gate
2 Chapel Crescent
3 The Chapel
4 Valley Water
5 The Tomb of the Soda Fountain King
6 Sylvan Water
7 Greeley Gravesite
8 Landscape Avenue
9 Fannie the Dog

❚❚It is the ambition of the New Yorker to live upon Fifth Avenue, to take his airings in the Park, and to sleep with his fathers in Green-Wood." So declared the *New York Times* in 1866. Today, Brooklyn's 1838 Green-Wood Cemetery is a great place to revel in the outdoors, with 438 scenic acres (177 ha) and countless ornate mausoleums.

❶ ★★ Main Gate. Green-Wood has five entrances, but this Gothic gate with spires that stretch church-like into the sky is by far the most spectacular. A New York City Historic Landmark, it was built from 1861 to 1865 by architect Richard M. Upjohn. At the information booth inside, you can pick up a free map of the grounds. It lists the many famous (and infamous) residents—some 600,000 in all. These include Samuel Morse, Henry Ward Beecher, Leonard Bernstein, Boss Tweed, Nathaniel Currier and James Ives, Jean-Michel Basquiat, and hundreds of Civil War soldiers. Self-guided walking tour booklets are also available for a fee. You will see NO PHOTOGRAPHY signs, but that rule isn't generally enforced unless you try to take pictures of mourners. ⏱ *2 hr. 500 25th St. (at Fifth Ave.), Brooklyn.* ☎ *718/768-7300. www.green-wood.com. Daily 8am–5pm (extended hours in summer). Trolley tours $15–$20. Subway: N/R to 25th St. in Brooklyn.*

❷ ★ Chapel Crescent. Green-Wood's grand chapel (see below) is surrounded by stunning tombs. The B. Stephens tomb is shaped like a small Egyptian pyramid. The Chambettaz tomb has an angel statue overlooking the crescent as well as symbols from the secret society of the Freemasons.

❸ ★★★ The Chapel. A few minutes' walk from the main gates is Green-Wood's crowning glory. The 1911 chapel is a relatively recent arrival, its design inspired by Tom Tower at Oxford's Christ Church college, the work of architect Christopher Wren in the 17th century. The multidomed structure is built entirely of Indiana limestone. The small interior frequently hosts readings and special exhibits that explore funerary art. Check the website for a calendar of events. ☎ *718/768-7300. www.green-wood.com.*

❹ Valley Water. Some of Green-Wood's ponds have been filled in to create new burial plots, but happily this stunning one remains. The avenue that curves around Valley Water is a treasure trove of 19th-century sculpture. Many of the monuments are partially draped by a carved "cloth." This popular Victorian Resurrectionist style reflected a belief that the body in the grave would rise on Judgment Day, when the cloth would fall away as if pulled back by the hand of God.

Green-Wood's elaborate main gate.

Governors Island: A Summer Weekend Treat

Open to the public on weekends from the end of May through September, this 172-acre (70-ha) island—just a short (free) ferry ride from lower Manhattan—is in the process of becoming a grand park, with a hammock grove, water features, public art, and a play lawn. There's also a historic district (the island is a former Army outpost and Coast Guard installation) and a national monument centered around two 1812 fortresses. But most come to the enchanting automobile-free island for the concerts, table-tennis championships, kite flying, and vintage amusement-park rides—or for a leisurely bike ride (BYO, or rent one for the day for $25). If you are traveling to New York in the summer or early fall, check the website for upcoming events. ☎ 212/440-2200. www.govisland.com. Ferries depart from Battery Maritime Building, Slip #7. Subway: 1 to South Ferry.

❺ ★ The Tomb of the Soda Fountain King. This towering work of sculpture is really just one giant tombstone: In 1870, it won the Mortuary Monument of the Year award. (Didn't know there was such a thing, did you?) This is the resting place of John Matthews, the man who invented the soda fountain—and that information is about the only thing not carved into it. Gargoyles, members of the Matthews family, and Matthews himself are all here.

Former military buildings on Governor's Island.

❻ Sylvan Water. This is the largest body of water in Green-Wood. It's surrounded by a series of tombs, some of which look large enough to house a (living) family.

❼ ★ Greeley Grave Site. Horace Greeley was an antislavery advocate who founded the *New York Tribune* and was a national figure. ("Go West, young man" is one of his famous aphorisms.) The views from his family plot are lovely.

❽ Landscape Avenue. This winding avenue offers memorable vistas and some great statuary.

❾ Fannie the Dog. Anyone who has ever loved a pet will relate to the engraving on the headstone of Fannie, sewing-machine inventor Elias Howe's pooch: "FROSTS OF WINTER NOR HEAT OF SUMMER / COULD MAKE HER FAIL IF MY FOOTSTEPS LED / AND MEMORY HOLDS IN ITS TREASURE CASKET / THE NAME OF MY DARLING WHO LIES DEAD." ●

Dining Best Bets

Best Places for a Carnivore
Keens $$$ *72 W. 36th St. (p 121);*
and Peter Luger $$$ *178 Broadway,
Brooklyn (p 123)*

Best Vegetarian
Pure Food and Wine $$ *54 Irving
Place (p 123)*

Best French
Le Bernardin $$$$ *55 W. 51st St.
(p 121)*

Best Cheap Eats
Gray's Papaya $ *2090 Broadway
(p 119)*

Best Burger
Burger Joint $ *119 W. 56th St.
(p 117)*

Best Chinese
Great NY Noodletown $ *28 Bowery
(p 119)*

Best Food Courts
Chelsea Market $ *75 Ninth Ave.
(p 117);* and Eataly $–$$ *200 Fifth
Ave. (p 119)*

Best Delis
Barney Greengrass $ *541 Amster-
dam Ave. (p 116);* and Katz's $ *205
E. Houston St. (p 121)*

Best Pizza
Keste $ *271 Bleecker St. (p 121)*

Best Seafood
Le Bernardin $$$$ *55 W. 51st St.
(p 119)*

Best Splurges
Eleven Madison Park $$$$ *11 Madison Ave. (p 122);* and Blue Hill $$$$
75 Washington Place (p 116)

Best Italian
Locanda Verde $$$ *377 Greenwich
St. (p 122)*

Best Indian
Tulsi $$$ *211 E. 46th St. (p 124)*

Best for Families
Carmine's $$ *2450 Broadway (p 117)*

Best New Restaurant
Lafayette $$$ *380 Lafayette St.
(p 121)*

*Previous page: Lamb burgers at the
Breslin.*

Downtown Dining

Midtown & Uptown Dining

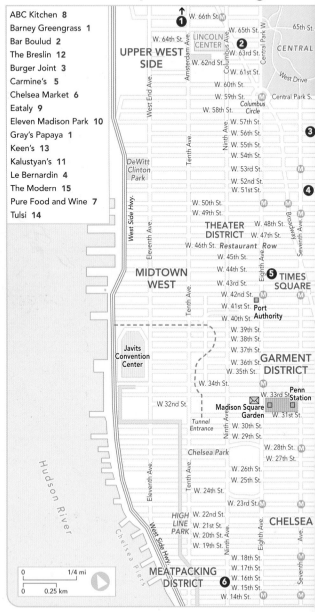

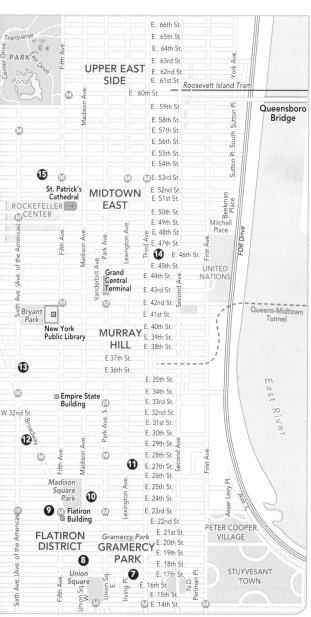

Restaurants A to Z

★★★ **ABC Kitchen** UNION SQUARE *NEW AMERICAN* Chef Jean-Georges Vongerichten has taken on the farm-to-table trend with this rustic yet elegant spot uniquely located in a high-end furniture store. Expect fresh, impeccably sourced ingredients and a delicious, impeccably prepared menu. It's comfort food for foodies. *ABC Carpet & Home, 35 E. 18th St. (at Broadway).* ☎ *212/475-5829. www.abckitchennyc.com. Main courses $21–$37. AE, DISC, MC, V. Lunch & dinner daily. Subway: 4/5/6/L/N/R to Union Sq.*

★★ **Babbo** WASHINGTON SQUARE *ITALIAN* A big star in celebrity chef Mario Batali's edible empire. Set in a warm, flower-filled town house, Babbo is lit from within with a special-occasion glow. The pasta-tasting menu is a smart choice. *110 Waverly Place (at Sixth Ave.).* ☎ *212/777-0303. www.babbonyc.com. Main courses $19–$29, 7-course tasting menus $69–$75. AE, MC, V. Dinner daily. Subway: A/C/E/F/B/D to 4th St.*

★★ **Bar Boulud** UPPER WEST SIDE *FRENCH COUNTRY* After a shaky start, this Lincoln Center–area restaurant from Daniel Boulud is firing on all cylinders. It specializes in house-made charcuterie, but the fish is cooked to perfection. A red-wine-braised flatiron steak melts like butter. High ceilings and mirrored walls make this long, narrow space look roomier—and brilliantly reflect the fashionable sorts who flock here. *1900 Broadway (btw. 63rd & 64th sts.).* ☎ *212/595-0303. www.danielnyc.com. Main courses $25–$33. AE, MC, V. Lunch & dinner daily, late-night supper Fri–Sat. Subway: 1 to 64th St.*

★ **Barney Greengrass** UPPER WEST SIDE *DELI* The Sturgeon King has been selling lox and bagels for a century at this favorite weekend brunch spot. The vintage counters and dairy case are beautiful. *541 Amsterdam Ave. (btw. 86th & 87th sts.).* ☎ *212/724-4707. www.barneygreengrass.com. Main courses $6–$19, smoked-fish platters $25–$45. AE, MC, V. Breakfast & lunch (or brunch) Tues–Sun. Subway: 1/9 to 86th St.*

★★★ **Blue Hill** GREENWICH VILLAGE *AMERICAN* This soothing, understated Village town-house space quietly goes about its business serving some of the most delicious food in town, with an

Authentic dim sum dumplings in Chinatown.

Inside the Breslin.

admirable sustainable-foods philosophy that travels beautifully from purveyor to plate. Chef Dan Barber coaxes the best out of the best ingredients. Even lowly Brussels sprouts become irresistible. *75 Washington Place (btw. Sixth Ave. & Washington Sq. W.).* ☎ *212/539-1776. www.bluehillfarm.com. Main courses $32–$36. AE, DC, MC, V. Dinner daily. Subway: B/D/F/M/A/C/E to W. 4th St.*

★★ The Breslin FLATIRON DISTRICT *GASTROPUB*   All dark wood, beveled glass, and cozy niches, this is a warm oasis for gastronomes and homesick Brits. Meat is the star, from the celebrated lamb burger to the pork-belly platter to house-made sausage. Even the boiled peanuts are fried in pork fat. *Ace Hotel, 16 W. 29th St. (at Broadway).* ☎ *212/679-1939. www.the breslin.com. Main courses $17–$29. AE, DC, DISC, MC, V. Breakfast, lunch & dinner Mon–Fri, brunch & dinner Sat–Sun. Subway: N/R to 28th St.*

★ Burger Joint MIDTOWN WEST *BURGERS*   Hidden behind a red curtain in the stylish lobby of Le Parker Meridien hotel, but far from a secret, lies a "joint" that might remind you of the greasy spoons of your college years. This one, however, far exceeds those with what may be the best burgers in the city.

And even better, the prices are more in keeping with a greasy spoon than a hotel of Le Parker Meridien's caliber. *119 W. 56th St. (btw. Sixth & Seventh aves.).* ☎ *212/708-7414. www.parkermeridien.com. Burgers $8–$9. Cash only. Lunch & dinner daily. Subway: F/N/Q/R to 57th St.*

★ kids Carmine's MIDTOWN WEST *ITALIAN*   A place this big and bustling doesn't have to have stellar food—but Carmine's does a lot of things very well. The vast dining room manages to feel both warm and festive, and the family-style portions of hearty pastas and Southern Italian favorites more than satisfy. *200 W. 44th St. (btw. Seventh & Eighth aves.).* ☎ *212/221-3800. www.carminesnyc.com. Main courses $25–$49. AE, DC, DISC, MC, V. Lunch & dinner daily. Subway: 1/2/3/7/9/A/C/E/S to 42th St./Times Sq.*

★★ Chelsea Market CHELSEA *FOOD COURT*   The standout cafes/food stalls in this wholesale/retail food market are ensconced in a cleverly restored former Nabisco biscuit factory. There's plenty of seating amid massive exposed pipes, a gushing "waterfall," and a million square feet of market space. The food is seriously good here:

Chelsea Market.

Eleven Madison Park.

top-notch Thai from **Chelsea Thai,** lobster rolls and sushi from the **Lobster Place,** pastas and pizzas from **Buon Italia,** and sustainably sourced comfort food at the Cleaver Co.'s **Green Table.** *75 Ninth Ave. (btw. 15th & 16th sts.). www.chelseamarket.com. Breakfast, lunch & dinner daily, depending on restaurant. Subway: A/C/E to 14th St.*

★★ **Dominick's** THE BRONX *ITALIAN* The dining room is small and slightly cramped. You may have a long wait for a table on weekend evenings. But hang in and you will be well taken care of by the skilled if taciturn waitstaff at this legendary spot, which has no menus and no checks. You want some clams to start? A salad or a stuffed artichoke maybe? Yes, yes, and yes. Follow with a sampling of perfect seafood pastas, buttery shrimp *franchese,* and a perfectly cooked steak. *2335 Arthur Ave. (btw. 187th St. & Crescent Ave.).* ☎ *718/733-2807. Main courses $10–$25. Cash only. Lunch & dinner Wed–Mon. Subway: B/D to 183rd St.*

★★ **The Dutch** SOHO *NEW AMERICAN* Andrew Carmellini's 2011 creation upped his chef credentials to practically Hall of Fame levels. The cuisine at the Dutch is hard to classify—is it a steakhouse? Italian? Asian fusion? Seafood? Or is it above categorizing? Whatever you want to call the fare, call it really good. And that's all that

New York's Pizza Universe

In my biased but expert opinion, there is no better town for pizza west of Naples than New York. A pizza place can be found on almost every city block, but I will be the first to admit that many of them aren't worth the 99¢ advertised for a slice. While in New York, stick to the standouts, of which there are many. Downtown has the great slice joint **Joe's Pizza** (7 Carmine St., at Bleecker St.; ☎ 212/255-3946). Frank Sinatra had pies from the wonderful old-school **Patsy's Pizzeria** (2287 First Ave., btw. 117th and 118th sts., East Harlem; ☎ 212/534-9783) shipped to Las Vegas. If you don't feel like a Nathan's hot dog at Coney Island, head to **Totonno's Pizzeria Napolitano** (1524 Neptune Ave., btw. W. 15th & W. 16th sts., Coney Island, Brooklyn; ☎ 718/372-8606), where the coal-fired oven has been churning out crispy charred-crust pizzas since 1924. In the Bronx's Little Italy on Arthur Ave. (p 3), **Trattoria Zero Otto Nove** (2357 Arthur Ave., at 186th St.; ☎ 718/220-1027) features innovative pizzas like butternut-squash puree with smoked mozzarella, made in a wood-burning brick oven.

Real New York pizza at John's.

matters. Despite the everyday crush, the quality of service is equal to the impressive food. *131 Sullivan St. (at Prince St.).* ☎ *212/677-6200. www.thedutchnyc.com. Main courses $19–$34. AE, DC, MC, V. Lunch & dinner daily, brunch Sat–Sun. Subway: C/E to Spring St.*

Eataly FLATIRON DISTRICT *ITALIAN* Opened to much fanfare in 2010, this bustling, dynamic Italian-centric marketplace has sit-down restaurants, standing-table *enotecas*, a raw-bar counter, a *rosticerria* (with daily roasted meat specials), a pizzeria, a *pasticerria*, a *gelateria*—even a rooftop beer garden. *See p 98.*

★★★ Eleven Madison Park

FLATIRON DISTRICT *FRENCH COUNTRY/AMERICAN* Chef Daniel Humm won the James Beard award for Best New York City Chef in 2010—and that's saying something. This gem from restaurateur Danny Meyer is set in a soaring Art Deco space. The two-story windows have spectacular views of the park at night. *11 Madison Ave. (at 24th St.).* ☎ *212/889-0905. www.eleven madisonpark.com. Tasting menu $195. AE, DC, DISC, MC, V. Lunch Mon–Sat, dinner daily. Subway: N/R/6 to 23rd St.*

★ Gray's Papaya UPPER WEST SIDE *HOT DOGS*

Unless you are heading to Coney Island for an original **Nathan's** hot dog, Gray's Papaya serves the best—and cheapest—dogs in the city. Open 24 hours, the Gray's outpost on the Upper West Side is an institution. The hot-dog stand's "recession special," which survives even when the economy is thriving, is a mere $4.95 and includes two hot dogs and your choice of a sweet papaya, orange, or piña-colada juice. *2090 Broadway (at 72nd St.).* ☎ *212/799-0243. Subway: 1/2/3 to 72nd St.*

★★ Great NY Noodletown

CHINATOWN *CHINESE* Don't be fooled by the run-down diner appearance; the food here may be the best in Chinatown. The seafood-based noodle soups are spectacular, the salt-baked shrimp is as good as you'll find anywhere, and the platters of roast pig, roast pork (yes, there is a difference), and spareribs on rice are irresistible. Whatever you order is very easy on the wallet, adding to Noodletown's immense appeal. *28 Bowery (at Bayard St.).* ☎ *212/349-0923. www. greatnynoodletown.com. Platters/ soups $6–$16. Cash only. Breakfast, lunch & dinner daily. Subway: N/R/6 to Canal St.*

Spices for sale at Kalustyan's.

★★ Hearth EAST VILLAGE *MEDI-TERRANEAN/ITALIAN* This warm East Villager is a favorite of diners and critics alike. It's all about fresh, seasonal local food cooked with tender loving care. *403 E. 12th St. (at First Ave.).* ☎ *646/602-1300. www. restauranthearth.com. Main courses $26–$30, 7-course tasting menu $72. AE, DISC, MC, V. Dinner daily. Subway: N/R/4/5/6 to Union Sq.*

John's Pizzeria of Bleecker Street kids GREENWICH VILLAGE *PIZZA* The decor in this longtime Bleecker Street favorite, founded in 1929, hasn't changed over the years: wooden booths, Olde Italy mural, and tin ceilings. The pizza

The pastrami sandwich at Katz's.

hasn't changed, either. The brick-oven pies are thin, crispy, and delicious. There's also a branch in Times Square (260 W. 44th St.; ☎ 212/391-7560). *278 Bleecker St. (btw. Sixth & Seventh aves.).* ☎ *212/243-1680. www.johnsbrick ovenpizza.com. Pizzas $12–$14, toppings $2. No credit cards. Lunch & dinner daily. Subway: A/C/E/B/D/F/M at W. 4th St.*

★ Kalustyan's MURRAY HILL *MIDDLE EASTERN MARKET/ CAFE* Downstairs is a Middle Eastern market, its wooden barrels filled with nuts, grains, herbs, and spices. Climb the stairs to the little cafe and order a sublime *mujadarra* (lentils and bulgur wheat cooked with caramelized onions) in a pita, fresh soup, or other homemade Indian specialties. *123 Lexington Ave. (btw. 27th and 28th sts.).* ☎ *212/685-3451. www.kalustyans. com. Platters/sandwiches $5–$8. AE, MC, V. Lunch daily. Subway: F to Second Ave.*

★ Katz's Delicatessen LOWER EAST SIDE *DELI* Founded in 1888, this homely, cacophonous space is one of the city's last great old-time delis. No one makes a better pastrami or brisket sandwich. Plus, you can see the spot where Meg Ryan performed her famous scene in

When Harry Met Sally. 205 E. Houston St. (at Ludlow St.). ☎ *212/254-2246. www.katzdeli.com. Sandwiches $3–$10, other items $5–$18. AE, MC, V. Breakfast, lunch & dinner daily. Subway: F to Second Ave.*

★★★ **Keens** MIDTOWN WEST
STEAK If you're searching for old New York, look no further than this 1885 survivor tucked away on a side street near Madison Square Garden. The space has always been wonderful; now the food is its equal. I had one of the best steaks I've ever eaten here. *72 W. 36th St. (at Sixth Ave.).* ☎ *212/947-3636. www.keens.com. Main courses $26–$57. AE, DC, DISC, MC, V. Lunch & dinner Mon–Fri, dinner Sat & Sun. Subway: 1/2/3/9 to 34th St./Penn Station.*

★★ **Keste** GREENWICH VILLAGE
PIZZA Invading John's Pizzeria's Bleecker Street turf is Neapolitan upstart Keste, which offers artisanal pizza following the strict guidelines of the Association of Neapolitan Pizza. This means the chefs use only the best ingredients for the more than 40 different creations—the worst thing about Keste is choosing your pie. *271 Bleecker St. (btw. Seventh Ave. & Carmine St.).* ☎ *212/243-1500. www.kestepizzeria.com. Pizza*

$10–$20. AE, MC, V. Lunch & dinner daily. Subway: A/B/C/D/E/F/M to W. 4th St.

★ **Lafayette** NOHO FRENCH
The most recent Andrew Carmellini (The Dutch, Locanda Verde) venture is this stylish, rustic French brasserie. Starting with the in-house bread from the adjoining bakery and the silky, sea-salt-sprinkled butter and continuing to the hearty duck au poivre, the treats here are plentiful and live up to the chef's very high standards. The place is bustling, as you would expect with a Carmellini-run restaurant, but the airy, exquisite room and well-thought-out seating make dining here a pleasure. *380 Lafayette St. (at Great Jones St.).* ☎ *212/533-3000. www.lafayetteny.com. Main courses $18–$38. AE, DC, MC, V. Breakfast, lunch & dinner daily. Subway: 6 to Bleecker St.*

★★★ **Le Bernardin** MIDTOWN WEST FRENCH/SEAFOOD Chef Eric Ripert is a giant on the NYC culinary scene and a master with seafood. The formal service is impeccable. *55 W. 51st St. (btw. Sixth & Seventh aves.).* ☎ *212/489-1515. www.le-bernardin.com. Prix-fixe dinner $130, tasting menu $150 ($240 w/ wine pairings). AE, DC,*

Keens's century-old dining room.

Outdoor dining at Pastis.

DISC, MC, V. Lunch Mon–Fri, dinner Mon–Sat. Subway: N/R to 49th St.; 1/9 to 50th St.

★★ **Legend Bar and Restaurant** CHELSEA *ASIAN FUSION* Legendary Szechuan food is created in this grand bi-level restaurant that attracts groups of dedicated spice worshippers. "Tears in Eyes" is the appropriate name for Legend's fiery mung-bean noodles and what you might experience if you dare order it. If you want to keep your eyes dry, settle for the braised whole fish with hot bean sauce. Whatever you choose here, you won't be disappointed. *88 Seventh Ave. (btw. 15th & 16th sts.).* ☎ 212/929-1819. www.legend restaurant88.com. *Main courses $9–$24. AE, MC, V. Lunch & dinner daily. Subway: 1/2/3 to 14th St.*

★★ **Locanda Verde** TRIBECA *ITALIAN* Chef Andrew Carmellini (The Dutch, Lafayette) became a celebrity chef after opening Locanda Verde—and for good reason. Here, he brings a culinary master's touch to simple, rustic Italian fare. This eatery—located in the Greenwich Hotel—is popular, so book early. The sheep's-milk ricotta sprinkled with sea salt and herbs slathered on crostini will make any reservation hassles quickly fade away. *377 Greenwich St. (at N. Moore St.).* ☎ 212/925-3797. www. locandaverdenyc.com. *Main courses $18–$32. AE, DISC, MC, V. Breakfast, lunch & dinner daily. Subway: 1 to Franklin St.*

★ **Lupa** GREENWICH VILLAGE *ITALIAN* This brick-lined homage to a Roman trattoria has been filled to capacity since it opened. The food is impeccable and often inventive, and the prices won't bankrupt you. It's part of the Batali/Bastianich empire. *170 Thompson St. (btw. Houston & Bleecker sts.).* ☎ 212/982-5089. www.lupa restaurant.com. *Main courses $13–$24. AE, MC, V. Lunch & dinner daily. Subway: B/D/F/M/A/C/E to W. 4th St.*

★★ **The Modern** MIDTOWN WEST *AMERICAN* Dining in this elegant space overlooking MoMA's sculpture garden makes you feel as if you're at the center of a very sophisticated urban universe—and you are. The food lives up to the setting, and the cross-section of New Yorkers crisply doing business makes this a great spot to see the local tribe in action. *The Museum of Modern Art, 9 W. 53rd St. (btw. Fifth & Sixth aves.).* ☎ 212/333-1220. www.themodernnyc.com. *4-course prix-fixe menu $98, 7-course tasting menu $155. AE, DC, DISC, MC, V. Lunch Mon–Fri, dinner Mon–Sat. Subway: E/M to Fifth Ave./53rd St.*

★ **Nyonya** LITTLE ITALY *MALAYSIAN* Spacious and bustling, this restaurant looks like a South Asian tiki hut. Try the Malaysian national dish, *roti canai* (an Indian pancake with a curry chicken dipping sauce). *199 Grand St. (btw. Mulberry & Mott sts.).* ☎ 212/619-0085. www.iloven-yonya.com. *Main courses $6–$23. No credit cards. Lunch & dinner daily. Subway: 6 to Spring St.*

Restaurant Week: Prix-Fixe Dining

Everyone loves a deal, and Restaurant Week is one of New York's best. It started more than a decade ago, when some of the city's best dining spots began to offer three courses for a fixed low price at lunch ($24) and dinner ($38). Now it's an institution that lasts for several weeks in January and July. Some restaurants offer prix-fixe menus year-round or have discounted menus on certain days or times. For example, the Lambs Club (p 26) has a $38 prix-fixe dinner menu. Check out **www.opentable.com** or **www.nycvisit.com** for more information on Restaurant Week and participating restaurants.

★ kids **Pastis** MEATPACKING DISTRICT *FRENCH BISTRO* This sunny, artful replication of a French bistro on a central Meatpacking District street has been packing 'em since it opened in 1999. The Provençal specialties, such as a classic tuna *niçoise* and Pernod-soaked *moules-frites*, will have you pining for a French *grandmère*. *9 Ninth Ave. (btw. Little W. 12th & 13th sts.).* ☎ *212/929-4844. www.pastisny.com. Main courses $19–$36. AE, MC, V. Breakfast, lunch (or brunch), dinner & late-night supper daily. Subway: A/C/E to 14th St.*

★ **Perilla** GREENWICH VILLAGE *AMERICAN* A TV reality-show alumnus runs this small but exciting Village restaurant. *Top Chef* 2006 winner Harold Dieterle is a talent; his menu is seasonal, but look for the spicy duck meatballs. *9 Jones St. (btw. W. 4th & Bleecker sts.).* ☎ *212/929-6868. www.perillanyc.com. Main courses $21–$28, 6-course tasting menu $80. AE, MC, V. Dinner daily, brunch Sat–Sun. Subway: A/C/E/B/D/F/M to W. 4th St.*

★★★ **Peter Luger Steakhouse** BROOKLYN *STEAK* This Brooklyn institution is porterhouse heaven. The meat cuts like butter, and the waiters are properly crusty. *178 Broadway (at Driggs Ave.), Brooklyn.* ☎ *718/387-7400. www.peterluger.com. Main courses $20–$35. Debit cards & checks with ID accepted. Lunch & dinner daily. Subway: J/M/Z to Marcy Ave.*

★ **Pure Food and Wine** GRAMERCY *RAW/VEGAN* The delicious food is a revelation at the standard-bearer of the raw-food movement, where nothing is cooked above 118°F (48°C). *54*

The classic New York bagel with lox, onions, and cream cheese.

Soul food at Sylvia's in Harlem.

Irving Place (at 17th St.). ☎ 212/477-1010. www.oneluckyduck.com. Main courses $24–$26. AE, MC, V. Lunch & dinner daily. Subway: L/N/R/4/5/6 to 14th St./Union Sq.

★★ **Recette** GREENWICH VILLAGE *NEW AMERICAN* Grazing is elevated to an art form at Recette. New-wave alchemy meets old-school techniques in the fashioning of snacks and small plates. How about Berkshire pork belly with rock shrimp, turnips, romesco, and sherry caramel? Finish with the deconstructed s'mores: graham-cracker ice cream, toasted marshmallows, and hot and spicy chocolate ganache. 328 W. 12th St. (at Greenwich St.). ☎ 212/414-3000. www.recettenyc.com. Plates $10–$38, chef's tasting menus $75–$100. AE, MC, V. Dinner Mon–Sat, brunch Sat–Sun. Subway: A/C/E/1/2/3 to 14th St.

Sylvia's HARLEM *SOUL FOOD* The late founder of Sylvia's, Sylvia Woods, built an empire (canned food products, fragrances, etc.) from what began as a street-front soul-food diner. Although now a bit touristy, the Sunday gospel brunch at her original Harlem restaurant is still a delight. 328 Lenox Ave. (btw. 126th & 127th sts.). ☎ 212/996-0660. www.sylviassoulfood.com. Main courses $9–$19. AE, DC, DISC, MC, V. Breakfast Mon–Fri, lunch & dinner daily. Subway: 2/3 to 125th St.

★ **Tulsi** MIDTOWN EAST *INDIAN* A star in the world of Indian cuisine, chef Hemant Mathur fully displays his estimable talents at Tulsi. With this venue in the heart of Midtown, fans can enjoy his legendary creations, such as shrimp and crab-stuffed *pappadum*, tandoor-grilled lamb chops, and the truly memorable Manchurian cauliflower. The chef's tasting menu, vegetarian or other, is the way to go here. 211 E. 46th St. (btw. Second & Third aves.). ☎ 212/888-0820. www.tulsiny.com. 7-course tasting menus $65. AE, MC, V. Lunch & dinner Mon–Sat. Subway: 4/5/6/7/S to 42nd-Grand Central. ●

OLD KING COLE

Nightlife Best Bets

Best **Old-School Atmosphere**
King Cole Bar, 2 E. 55th St. (p 132)

Best **Choice of Single-Malt Scotches**
dba, 41 First Ave. (p 131)

Best **Place to Bowl & Sip a Martini**
Bowlmor Lanes, 110 University Place (p 130)

Best **Piano Bar**
Brandy's Piano Bar, 235 E. 84th St. (p 134)

Best **Cocktails**
Pegu Club, 77 W. Houston St. (p 132)

Best **Hotel Bar**
Bemelmans, The Carlyle, 35 E. 76th St. (p 130)

Best **Museum Bar**
Roof Garden, Metropolitan Museum of Art, 1000 Fifth Ave. (p 132)

Best **Vodka Selection**
Russian Samovar, 256 W. 52nd St. (p 133)

Best **Bar with a View**
Jimmy, 15 Thompson St. (p 131)

Best **Bar to Hear the Written Word**
KGB Bar, 85 E. 4th St. (p 132)

Take the L Train: Billyburg Bars

Just over the bridge in Brooklyn, Williamsburg mushroomed when artists, young professionals, and expats from the Lower East Side poured in to escape soaring Manhattan rents. It's a happening neighborhood, with a multicultural mix, big living lofts, and railroad apartments. And bars. To check out some of the city's freshest, you only need to take a short ride from 14th Street in Manhattan to Lorimer Street in Brooklyn on the L train. **Union Pool** (www.union-pool.com) is a welcoming bar with a large outdoor space, velvet lounges, and a post-hipster crowd. **Pete's Candy Store** (www.petescandystore.com) is a wonderful tavern with live music, trivia, spelling-bee nights, and a Sunday backyard barbecue. If you want to see a hot band in a top-notch setting, the **Music Hall of Williamsburg** (www.musichallofwilliamsburg.com)—a sister club to the Bowery Ballroom and Mercury Lounge in Manhattan—is a good bet.

Previous page: Bellying up to the King Cole Bar.

Downtown Nightlife

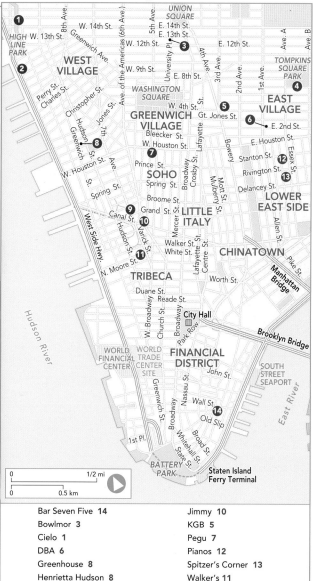

Bar Seven Five **14**	Jimmy **10**
Bowlmor **3**	KGB **5**
Cielo **1**	Pegu **7**
DBA **6**	Pianos **12**
Greenhouse **8**	Spitzer's Corner **13**
Henrietta Hudson **8**	Walker's **11**
Jane Ballroom **2**	Zum Schneider **4**

Midtown & Uptown Nightlife

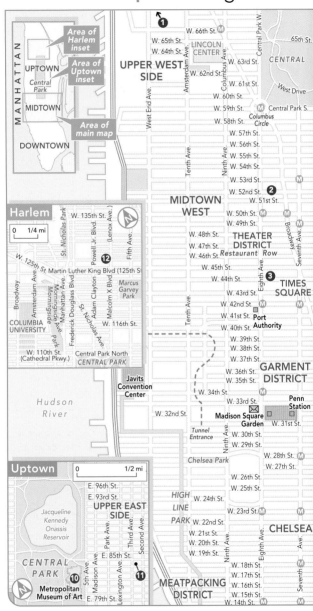

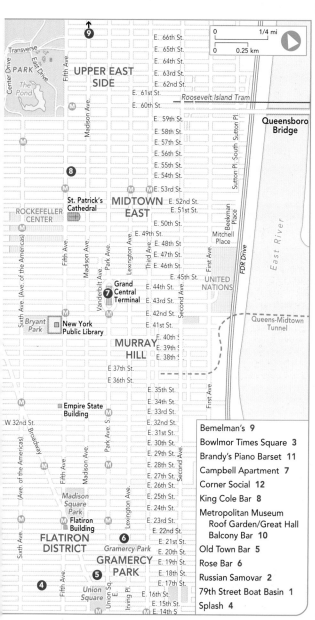

0	1/4 mi
0	0.25 km

Transverse

Center Drive

PARK

East Drive

The Pond

Fifth Ave.

UPPER EAST SIDE

Madison Ave.

E. 66th St.
E. 65th St.
E. 64th St.
E. 63rd St.
E. 62nd St.
E. 61st St.
E. 60th St.
E. 59th St.
E. 58th St.
E. 57th St.
E. 56th St.
E. 55th St.
E. 54th St.
E. 53rd St.
E. 52nd St.
E. 51st St.
E. 50th St.
E. 49th St.
E. 48th St
E. 47th St.
E. 46th St.
E. 45th St.

Roosevelt Island Tram

Sutton Pl. South   Sutton Pl.

Queensboro Bridge

Beekman Place

Mitchell Place

First Ave.

FDR Drive

East River

ROCKEFELLER CENTER

Fifth Ave.

Madison Ave.

Park Ave.

Lexington Ave.

Third Ave.

Vanderbilt Ave.

St. Patrick's Cathedral

MIDTOWN EAST

Grand Central Terminal

E. 44th St
E. 43rd St.
E. 42nd St.
E. 41st St.

UNITED NATIONS

Second Ave.

Sixth Ave. (Ave. of the Americas)

Bryant Park

New York Public Library

MURRAY HILL

E. 40th S
E. 39th S
E. 38th S
E. 37th St.
E. 36th St.

Queens-Midtown Tunnel

First Ave.

Empire State Building

W 32nd St.

Broadway

(Ave. of the Americas)

Fifth Ave.

Madison Ave.

Park Ave. S.

Lexington Ave.

Second Ave.

E. 35th St.
E. 34th St.
E. 33rd St.
E. 32nd St.
E. 31st St.
E. 30th St.
E. 29th St.
E. 28th St.
E. 27th St.
E. 26th St.
E. 25th St.
E. 24th St.
E. 23rd St.
E. 22nd St.
E. 21st St.
E. 20th St.
E. 19th St.
E. 18th St.
E. 17th St.
E. 16th St.
E. 15th St.
E. 14th S

Madison Square Park

Flatiron Building

FLATIRON DISTRICT

Sixth Ave.

Fifth Ave.

Gramercy Park

GRAMERCY PARK

Union Sq.

Union Square

Irving Pl.

Bemelman's **9**

Bowlmor Times Square **3**

Brandy's Piano Barset **11**

Campbell Apartment **7**

Corner Social **12**

King Cole Bar **8**

Metropolitan Museum Roof Garden/Great Hall Balcony Bar **10**

Old Town Bar **5**

Rose Bar **6**

Russian Samovar **2**

79th Street Boat Basin **1**

Splash **4**

Nightlife A to Z

Bar Seven Five.

Bars & Cocktail Lounges

★★ **Bar Seven Five** FINANCIAL DISTRICT This dazzling lounge in the Andaz Wall Street hotel has a percolating happy hour, a fizzy cocktail of Wall Streeters, hotel guests, and a growing cadre of downtown locals. *Andaz Wall Street, 75 Wall St. (at Water St.).* ☎ *212/590-1234. www.newyork.wallstreet. andaz.hyatt.com. Subway: 2/3 to Wall St./William St.; 4/5 to Wall St.*

Carnival at Bowlmor Lanes.

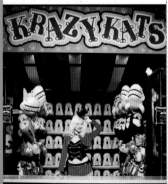

★ **Bemelmans Bar** UPPER EAST SIDE A playful mural by illustrator Ludwig Bemelmans, author of the *Madeline* children's books, decorates this old-school white-gloved lounge in the **Carlyle** hotel. Perched at one of the tables set around a piano that tinkles with show standards, you might even forget to check your cell phone while sipping perfectly made classic cocktails in this treasure from another era. *35 E. 76th St. (at Madison Ave.).* ☎ *212/744-1600. Subway: 6 to 77th St.*

★★ **Bowlmor Lanes** UNION SQUARE This 1938 bowling alley has gone mod, with candy-colored lanes, martinis, glow-in-the-dark bowling, and DJs playing house and techno music. *110 University Place (btw. 12th & 13th sts.).* ☎ *212/255-8188. www.bowlmor. com. Subway: 4/5/6/L/N/R to 14th St./Union Sq.*

★★ **Bowlmor Times Square** TIMES SQUARE This 90,000-square-foot mega-entertainment complex in Times Square has 50 bowling lanes in seven New York–themed sections, splashy carnival games, and an epic sports bar with stadium seating. *Times Square Building, 229 W. 44th St. (btw. Seventh & Eighth aves.).* ☎ *212/680-0012. www. bowlmor.com. Subway: R/S/W/1/2/3/7 to 42nd St./Times Sq.*

★★ The Campbell Apartment

MIDTOWN EAST   Tucked away on the mezzanine level of Grand Central Terminal, this cozy lounge recalls the glamour of 1920s New York. The luxurious setting boasts intricate architectural details, an enormous fireplace, and a high, beamed ceiling. It's a champagne-worthy place, but even just sipping a beer in this "apartment" will make you feel like a tycoon. *15 Vanderbilt Ave. (btw. 42nd & 43rd sts.).* ☎ *212/953-0409. Subway: 4/5/6/7/S to Grand Central-42nd St.*

Corner Social HARLEM   It's a great day (or night) in Harlem when, after wandering the fascinating and historic streets, you can relax at what is now one of the area's social hubs. The beer and cocktail list is extensive and innovative, while the menu offers many tempting creations. On weekends,

a DJ spins into the wee hours. *321 Lenox Ave. (at 126th St.).* ☎ *212/510-8552. www.cornersocialnyc.com. Subway: 2/3 to 125th St.*

★★ dba EAST VILLAGE   Lounges dominate the city, but dba is a refreshing change of pace. It's an unpretentious neighborhood bar—a beer- or whiskey-lover's dream. The collection of single-malt scotches is phenomenal. *41 First Ave. (btw. 2nd & 3rd sts.).* ☎ *212/475-5097. www.drinkgood stuff.com. Subway: F to Second Ave.*

★★ Jane Hotel Ballroom WEST VILLAGE   This baronial lounge is the size of a ballroom but feels more like the tapestried grand room of a Victorian manor. *113 Jane St. (at West End Hwy.).* ☎ *212/924-6700. www.thejanenyc.com. Subway: A/C/E to 14th St.*

Jimmy SOHO   On the roof of the James Hotel, this glass-walled lounge offers spectacular downtown views. But your stargazing might be eclipsed (or maybe enhanced) by cocktail creations featuring house-made bitters and syrups with herbs from the hotel's organic garden. There is a lot of

Behind the bar at dba.

The Jane Hotel Ballroom.

beauty at Jimmy, both in the lush decor and in the bar's attractive clientele. *15 Thompson St. (at Grand St.). ☎ 212/201-9118. www.jimmy soho.com. Subway 1 to Canal St.*

KGB Bar EAST VILLAGE Formerly a Ukrainian social club, this 2nd- floor bar decorated in Communist memorabilia is now a mecca for some of the city's best author readings, be it fiction, nonfiction, or poetry. There's never a cover, and the drinks are more than affordable. *85 E. 4th St. (btw. Second & Third aves.). ☎ 212/505-3360. Subway: 6 to Astor Place.*

★★ King Cole Bar MIDTOWN EAST The Bloody Mary was born here, in the tony St. Regis Hotel. The Maxfield Parrish mural alone is worth the price of a classic cocktail (but egads, what a price!). It's a small but memorable spot. *2 E. 55th St. (at Fifth Ave.). ☎ 212/744-4300. www.kingcolebar.com. Subway: E to Fifth Ave./53rd St.*

★★ Metropolitan Museum Roof Garden/Great Hall Balcony Bar UPPER EAST SIDE Every Friday and Saturday night from 4 to 8:30pm, the mezzanine level of the Met's lobby transforms into a lounge with live classical music. When the weather warms, take the elevator up to the **Roof Garden** for drinks with sumptuous views of the park. *Metropolitan Museum of Art, 1000 Fifth Ave. (at 82nd St.). ☎ 212/535-7710. www. metmuseum.org. Subway: 4/5/6 to 86th St.*

Old Town Bar FLATIRON DISTRICT You know a bar is old when the burgers and fries are shuttled from the kitchen via a working dumbwaiter. This place was immortalized by David Letterman in the opening credits of his late-night show but has been around a lot longer than Dave. It's a hangout for the literary set, but you don't have to be a wordsmith to enjoy a beer here. *45 E. 18th St. (btw. Broadway & Park Ave. S.). ☎ 212/529-6713. www.oldtownbar.com. Subway: 4/5/6/L/N/R/Q to 14th St./Union Sq.*

★★ Pegu Club SOHO Self-described "gatekeepers of classic cocktail culture," the Pegu Club brings uptown to downtown in this sleek and polished venue. *77 W. Houston St., 2nd floor (at W. Broadway). ☎ 212/473-PEGU (473-7348). www.peguclub.com. Subway: 6/F/M to Bleecker St./Lafayette St.*

★★ Pianos LOWER EAST SIDE This multilevel former piano store gets high marks both as a bar and as a music venue. On any given night, three or four different performances may be going on. *158 Ludlow St.* ☎ *212/505-3733. www.pianosnyc. com. Subway: F/M to Second Ave.*

★★ **Rose Bar** GRAMERCY PARK Ian Schrager's 2006 head-to-toe renovation of the old Gramercy Park Hotel included the imaginative redesign of the bar by artist Julian Schnabel; it's like the great room in the country estate of some slightly nutty 21st-century Venetian prince. *2 Lexington Ave. (at Gramercy Park N.).* ☎ *212/920-3300. www.gramercy parkhotel.com. Subway: 6 to 23rd St.*

Russian Samovar MIDTOWN WEST   With more than 20 house-made infused vodkas to sample, this Theater District legend could make it difficult to get to the theater. The kitschy Russian interpretations of pop standards played on a white baby grand add to the dizzying effect of the vodkas. You might need to order a side dish of caviar with blinis to steady yourself. *256 W. 52nd St. (btw. Broadway & Eighth Ave).* ☎ *212/757-0168. www. russiansamovar.com. Subway: C/E to 50th St.*

★★ **79th Street Boat Basin** UPPER WEST SIDE   When spring finally arrives, nature-starved New Yorkers flock here to sip beer on the outdoor patio, mingle under limestone arches, and gaze out at the Hudson River. This is as much a casual restaurant as it is a bar, with hamburgers, hot dogs, and "garden burgers" sizzling on an outdoor grill. *79th Street Boat Basin, 79th St. & the Hudson River.* ☎ *212/496-5542. www.boatbasin cafe.com. Subway: 1 to 79th St.*

★ **Spitzer's Corner** LOWER EAST SIDE   This atmospheric American gastropub was named for the dress shop that occupied the space for 50 years—a nod to the Lower East Side's storied history. Spitzer's has 40 craft beers on tap and an extensive collection of bottled beers, excellent wines by the glass, and a full bar. A seasonal menu features creative twists on classic comfort foods. *101 Rivington St. (at Ludlow St.).* ☎ *212/228-0027. www.spitzerscorner.com. Subway: F to Delancey St; J/M/Z to Essex St.*

Walker's TRIBECA   Before TriBeCa commanded some of the top real-estate bucks per square foot, Walker's was there to serve a working man a cold brew and a burger. It's still there and still retains its charm, with cozy tables, a tin ceiling, and a long, conversation-inviting bar. *16 N. Moore St. (at Varick St.).* ☎ *212/941-0142. www. walkersnyc.com. Subway: 1 to Franklin St.*

The mural at the King Cole Bar.

Organic Bloody Marys at Spitzer's Corner.

Zum Schneider EAST VILLAGE
Just what Alphabet City needed: a genuine indoor Bavarian beer garden. With its long tables and bench seating, this is a *sehr gut* place to go with a group. *107 Ave. C (at 7th St.).* ☎ *212/598-1098. www.zum schneider.com. Subway: F to Second Ave.; L to First Ave.*

Dance Clubs

★ **Cielo** MEATPACKING DISTRICT
This ultracool space offers top DJs, a state-of-the-art sound system, and an electric ambience sans the snooty attitude (and dumbed-down crowds). *18 Little W. 12th St. (btw. Ninth Ave. & Washington St.).* ☎ *212/645-5700. www.cieloclub. com. $10–$20 cover. Subway: A/C/E to 14th St.*

Greenhouse GREENWICH
VILLAGE   An eco-friendly dance club? Who knew! Let your conscience be eased while partying to house, electronic, and hip-hop in this LEED-certified space. Check the website for special events and parties open to the public. *150 Varick St. (at Vandam St.).* ☎ *646/862-6117. www.greenhouseusa.com. Subway: 1 to Houston St.*

The Gay & Lesbian Scene

★★ **Brandy's Piano Bar** UPPER
EAST SIDE   The crowd is a mix of gay and straight, men and women, at this intimate piano bar. It's friendly and relaxed—so much so that the talented waitstaff who do most of the singing don't mind when patrons join in. *235 E. 84th St. (btw. Second & Third aves.).* ☎ *212/650-1944. www. brandyspianobar.com. Subway: 4/5/6 to 86th St.*

★★ **Flaming Saddles** HELLS
KITCHEN   Yee-haw! This country-western bar is Coyote Ugly reversed, with hot, shirtless male bartenders dancing atop the bar. Along with hunky guys, this place attracts a lot of bachelorette parties, but there's one rule: no "woo-hooing" female customers! *739 Ninth Ave. (at 39th St.).* ☎ *212/713-0481. Subway: C, E to 50th St.*

★ **Henrietta Hudson** WEST
VILLAGE   This popular ladies' lounge has been calling out to lipstick lesbians since 1991. The theme nights pack the house. *438 Hudson St. (at Morton St.).* ☎ *212/924-3347. www.henriettahudson. com. Subway: 1 to Houston St.* ●

Arts & Entertainment **Best Bets**

Most **Unusual Venue**
Bargemusic, *Fulton Ferry Landing, Brooklyn* (p 141)

Best **Free Concerts**
New York Philharmonic Concerts in the Park, *Central Park* (p 141)

Best **World Music**
S.O.B.'s, *204 Varick St.* (p 146)

Best **Historic Venue**
Apollo Theater, *253 W. 125th St.* (p 142)

Best **Food at a Club**
Jazz Standard, *116 E. 27th St.* (p 144)

Best **Classical Dance Troupe**
New York City Ballet, *Lincoln Center, Broadway & 64th St.* (p 141)

Best **Modern Dance Troupe**
Alvin Ailey American Dance Theater, *Joan Weill Center for Dance, 405 W. 55th St.* (p 141)

Best **Author Readings**
92nd Street Y, *1395 Lexington Ave.* (p 142)

Best **Repertory Theater Group**
New York Gilbert & Sullivan Players, *Symphony Space, 2537 Broadway* (p 147)

Best **New Comedians**
Gotham Comedy Club, *34 W. 22nd St.* (p 147)

Best **Rock-'n'-Roll Bar**
Mercury Lounge, *217 E. Houston St.* (p 145)

Most **Unforgettable Visual Spectacle**
Metropolitan Opera, *Lincoln Center, Broadway & 64th St.* (p 146)

Best **Jazz Club**
Smoke, *2751 Broadway* (p146)

Best **Find**
Paris Blues, *2021 Adam Clayton Powell Blvd.* (p 145)

Most **Cutting-Edge Major Venue**
Brooklyn Academy of Music, *30 Lafayette Ave., Brooklyn* (p 142)

Best **Place to See Shakespeare**
Public Theater, *425 Lafayette St.* (p 143)

Best **Church Concert Series**
Church of the Transfiguration, *1 E. 29th St.* (p 142)

Previous page: Louis C.K. performing at Carolines.

Downtown A&E

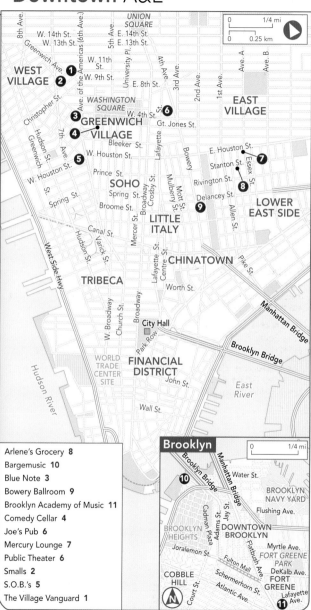

Arlene's Grocery 8
Bargemusic 10
Blue Note 3
Bowery Ballroom 9
Brooklyn Academy of Music 11
Comedy Cellar 4
Joe's Pub 6
Mercury Lounge 7
Public Theater 6
Smalls 2
S.O.B.'s 5
The Village Vanguard 1

Midtown & Uptown A&E

MANHATTAN

Area of Harlem inset
Area of Uptown inset
Central Park
MIDTOWN
Area of main map
DOWNTOWN

UPPER WEST SIDE

CENTRAL

W. 66th St.
W. 65th St. ❶
❷
W. 64th St.
LINCOLN CENTER
W. 62nd St.
W. 61st St.
W. 60th St.
W. 59th St. Central Park S.
W. 58th St. Columbus Circle
W. 57th St.
W. 56th St. ❹
W. 55th St. ❸ ❺
W. 54th St.
W. 53rd St.
W. 52nd St.
W. 51st St. ❻
MIDTOWN WEST ❼
W. 50th St.
W. 49th St.
THEATER DISTRICT
W. 48th St.
W. 47th St.
W. 46th St. Restaurant Row
W. 45th St.
W. 44th St. ❽ TIMES SQUARE
W. 43rd St.
W. 42nd St. ❾
W. 41st St. Port
W. 40th St. Authority
W. 39th St.
W. 38th St.
W. 37th St.
W. 36th St. GARMENT
W. 35th St. DISTRICT
W. 34th St.
W. 33rd St. Penn Station
Madison Square Garden ❿
W. 31st St.
W. 30th St.
W. 29th St.
W. 28th St.
W. 27th St.
W. 26th St.
W. 25th St.
W. 24th St.
W. 23rd St. ⓫
CHELSEA
W. 22nd St.
W. 21st St.
W. 20th St.
W. 19th St.
W. 18th St. ⓬
W. 17th St.
W. 16th St.
W. 15th St.
MEAT-PACKING DISTRICT

65th St.
Central Park W.
Columbus Ave.
West Drive
Amsterdam Ave.
West End Ave.
Tenth Ave.
Ninth Ave.
Eighth Ave.
Broadway
Seventh Ave.
Tunnel Entrance
Chelsea Park
HIGH LINE PARK
Seventh Ave.

Uptown

0 ———— 1/2 mi

❿⑲ W. 96th St.
⑳
W. 90th St.
W. 86th St.
UPPER WEST SIDE
W. 79th St.
Broadway
Amsterdam Ave.
Columbus Ave.
Central Park West

E. 96th St.
E. 93rd St.
E. 92nd St. ㉑
UPPER EAST SIDE
E. 86th St.
E. 79th St.

Jacqueline Kennedy Onassis Reservoir
CENTRAL PARK
Metropolitan Museum of Art
American Museum of Natural History

5th Ave.
Madison Ave.
Park Ave.
Lexington Ave.

Harlem

0 ———— 1/2 mi

W. 155th St.
Trinity Park
Jackie Robinson Park
Yankee Stadium
W. 145th St.
138th St.
St. Nicholas Park
W. 135th St.
Sheltering Arms Park
W. 125th St.
Morningside Park
COLUMBIA UNIVERSITY
MEAT-PACKING DISTRICT

Hudson River
Henry Hudson Pkwy.
Riverside Park
Riverside Dr.
Broadway
Amsterdam Ave.
Convent Ave.
St. Nicholas Ave.
Frederick Douglass Blvd.
Adam Clayton Powell Jr. Blvd.
Malcolm X Blvd.
Lenox Ave.
Marcus Garvey Park
E. 125th St. ㉒ ㉓
Harlem River
87
9A

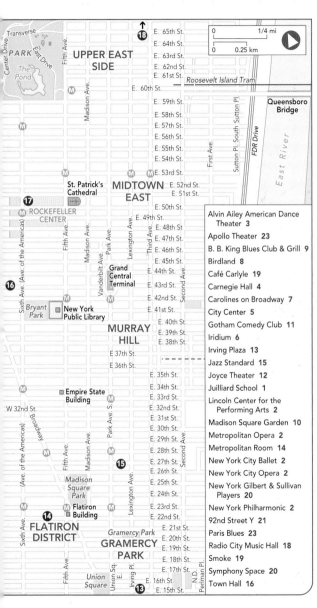

Transverse
Center Drive
East Drive
PARK
The
Pond

UPPER EAST
SIDE

E. 65th St.
E. 64th St.
E. 63rd St.
E. 62nd St.
E. 61st St.

Roosevelt Island Tram

E. 60th St.

E. 59th St.
E. 58th St.
E. 57th St.
E. 56th St.
E. 55th St.
E. 54th St.
E. 53rd St.

Queensboro
Bridge

St. Patrick's
Cathedral

MIDTOWN
EAST

E. 52nd St.
E. 51st St.
E. 50th St.

ROCKEFELLER
CENTER

E. 49th St.
E. 48th St.
E. 47th St.
E. 46th St.
E. 45th St.
E. 44th St.
E. 43rd St.
E. 42nd St.
E. 41st St.

Grand
Central
Terminal

Bryant
Park

New York
Public Library

MURRAY
HILL

E. 40th St.
E. 39th St.
E. 38th St.

E. 37th St.
E. 36th St.

E. 35th St.
E. 34th St.
E. 33rd St.
E. 32nd St.
E. 31st St.
E. 30th St.
E. 29th St.
E. 28th St.
E. 27th St.
E. 26th St.
E. 25th St.
E. 24th St.
E. 23rd St.
E. 22nd St.
E. 21st St.
E. 20th St.
E. 19th St.
E. 18th St.
E. 17th St.
E. 16th St.
E. 15th St.

Empire State
Building

Madison
Square
Park

Flatiron
Building

FLATIRON
DISTRICT

Gramercy Park

GRAMERCY
PARK

Union
Square

Alvin Ailey American Dance
  Theater **3**
Apollo Theater **23**
B. B. King Blues Club & Grill **9**
Birdland **8**
Café Carlyle **19**
Carnegie Hall **4**
Carolines on Broadway **7**
City Center **5**
Gotham Comedy Club **11**
Iridium **6**
Irving Plaza **13**
Jazz Standard **15**
Joyce Theater **12**
Juilliard School **1**
Lincoln Center for the
  Performing Arts **1**
Madison Square Garden **10**
Metropolitan Opera **2**
Metropolitan Room **14**
New York City Ballet **2**
New York City Opera **2**
New York Gilbert & Sullivan
  Players **20**
New York Philharmonic **2**
92nd Street Y **21**
Paris Blues **23**
Radio City Music Hall **18**
Smoke **19**
Symphony Space **20**
Town Hall **16**

Broadway Theaters

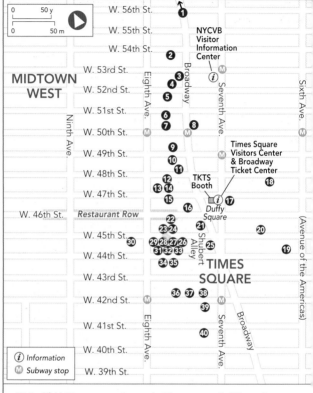

A&E A to Z

Classical Music

★ **Bargemusic** BROOKLYN Talk about original—this permanently docked barge at the foot of the Brooklyn Bridge is a primo chamber music concert hall. The intimate space hosts string quartets, world folk songs, and piano sonatas. *At Fulton Ferry Landing (just south of the Brooklyn Bridge), Brooklyn.* ☎ *718/624-2083. www.bargemusic. org. Tickets $15–$45. Subway: 2/3 to Clark St.; A/C to High St.*

★★★ **Juilliard School** LINCOLN CENTER America's premier music school sponsors more than 500 concerts a year, most at no charge. *60 Lincoln Center Plaza (Broadway at 65th St.).* ☎ *212/799-5000. www. juilliard.edu. Free admission to most shows, select performances at local jazz clubs $25. Subway: 1 to 66th St.*

★★★ **New York Philharmonic** LINCOLN CENTER Founded in 1842, this is one of the most talented symphonies on the planet. The summertime **Concerts in the Park** in Central Park are magical evenings of music and fireworks. *At*

Avery Fisher Hall, Lincoln Center, Broadway & 65th St. ☎ *212/875-5656 for audience services, 212/875-5030 for box office information, or 212/721-6500 for tickets. www. nyphil.org. Tickets $32–$133. Subway: 1/ to 66th St.*

Dance

★★ **Alvin Ailey American Dance Theater** MIDTOWN WEST This world-renowned modern-dance company's home is the eight-floor Joan Weill Center for Dance, the largest facility dedicated to dance in the country. *405 W. 55th St. (at Ninth Ave.).* ☎ *212/405-9000. www.alvinailey. org. Tickets $33–$78. Subway: 1/2/3/A/C to 59 St./Columbus Circle.*

★★ **City Center** MIDTOWN WEST The sightlines are terrific from all corners in this theater, where you can see innovative dance works, the Tony award–winning *Encores! Great American Musicals in Concert* series, or productions from the Manhattan Theatre Club. *131 W. 55th St. (btw. Sixth & Seventh aves.).* ☎ *877/247-0430. www.citycenter.org. Tickets $10–$150. Subway: F/N/Q/R/W to 57th St.; B/D/E to Seventh Ave.*

★★ **Joyce Theater** CHELSEA Built as a movie house, the Art Deco Joyce has become a splendid modern dance center. Its sister theater, the **Joyce SoHo** (155 Mercer St.), is a former firehouse and hosts experimental works. *175 Eighth Ave. (at 19th St.).* ☎ *212/691-9740. www.joyce.org. Tickets $10–$39. Subway: C/E to 23rd St.; 1 to 18th St.*

★★★ **New York City Ballet** LINCOLN CENTER The legendary George Balanchine founded this

Smoke Jazz and Supper Club.

The Allen Room at Lincoln Center.

stellar company. *At the New York State Theater, Lincoln Center, Broadway & 64th St.* ☎ *212/870-5570. www.nycballet.com. Tickets $20–$135. Subway: 1 to 66th St.*

Landmark Venues

★★★ Apollo Theater HARLEM
A legendary institution, with annual jazz concerts and a popular Amateur Night on Wednesdays. Check out www.apollotheater.org to see its comedy, dance, and other offerings. *See p 65.*

★★★ Brooklyn Academy of Music BROOKLYN Just 25 minutes by subway from Midtown,

BAM is the place for cutting-edge theater, opera, dance, and music. *30 Lafayette Ave. (off Flatbush Ave.), Brooklyn.* ☎ *718/636-4100. www.bam.org. Ticket prices vary. Subway: 2/3/4/5/B/D/M/N/Q/R to Atlantic Ave./Barclays Center.*

★★★ Carnegie Hall MIDTOWN
WEST   Perhaps the world's most famous performance space, Carnegie Hall features everything from orchestral classics to solo sitar. The **Isaac Stern Auditorium,** the 2,800-seat main hall, welcomes visiting orchestras from around the world. There's also the intimate 270-seat **Weill Recital Hall** and the ornate

Heavenly Sounds

New York churches may play traditional hymns during their religious services, but many also host afternoon and evening concerts in a variety of secular styles, from classical to opera, from instrumental to thrilling soloists. And the price is right: A few concerts require tickets, but most have a "requested donation" from $2 to $10. Check the websites for schedules. Some of the best include **Church of the Transfiguration** (1 E. 29th St.; www.littlechurch.org), **St. Bart's** (325 Park Ave.; www.stbarts.org), **St. Paul's Chapel and Trinity Church** (p 17), **the Cathedral of St. John the Divine** (p 65), and **St. Ignatius Loyola** (980 Park Ave.; www.stignatiusloyola.org).

underground 600-seat **Zankel Hall.** Tickets for the 1-hour tours (offered Oct–May) are available at the box office. ⏱ *1 hr. (for tour). 881 Seventh Ave. (at 56th St.).* ☎ *212/247-7800. www.carnegiehall.org. Ticket prices vary. Tours $10 adults, $8 students & seniors, $4 children 12 & under. Tours Mon–Fri 11:30am, 12:30pm, 2pm & 3pm; Sat 11:30am & 12:30pm; Sun 12:30pm. Subway: A/B/C/D/1 to Columbus Circle; N/Q/R/W to 57th St./Seventh Ave.*

★★★ Lincoln Center for the Performing Arts UPPER WEST

SIDE   A multimillion-dollar project has thoroughly modernized the concert halls and performance spaces of this world-famous arts complex. See listings for the **Juilliard School** (p 140), **New York Philharmonic** (p 140), **New York City Ballet** (p 141), **Metropolitan Opera** (p 146), and **New York City Opera** (p 146) for more information. *10 Lincoln Center Plaza (Broadway from 62nd–66th sts.).* ☎ *212/875-5456. www.lincolncenter.org. Ticket prices vary. Subway: 1 to 66th St.*

Madison Square Garden GAR-

MENT DISTRICT   The most famous names in popular music play this cavernous 20,000-seat arena. *Seventh Ave. (from 31st–33rd sts.).* ☎ *212/465-MSG1 (465-6741). www.thegarden.com. Ticket prices vary. Subway: A/C/E/1/2/3 to 34th St.*

★★ 92nd Street Y UPPER EAST

SIDE   Forget what you know about the YMCA—this Jewish community center offers concerts, literary readings, and superb cultural events with the top newsmakers of the day. *1395 Lexington Ave. (at 92nd St.).* ☎ *212/415-5500. www.92y.org. Ticket prices vary. Subway: 4/5/6 to 86th St.; 6 to 96th St.*

★★ Public Theater NOHO

Come here for groundbreaking stagings of Shakespeare's plays as

A street fair held by 92nd Street Y.

well as new plays, classical dramas, and solo performances. *425 Lafayette St. (btw. Astor Place & E. 4th St.).* ☎ *212/539-8500. www.publictheater.org. Ticket prices vary. Subway: 6 to Astor Place.*

★★ Radio City Music Hall

MIDTOWN WEST   This stunning 6,200-seat Art Deco theater is home to the annual Christmas Spectacular and the Rockettes. *See p 8.*

★ Symphony Space UPPER

WEST SIDE   Now in its 35th year, this innovative institution includes the **Peter Jay Sharp Theatre** and the **Leonard Nimoy Thalia Theater** and offers a varied program of dance, film, readings, and music. *2537 Broadway (at 95th St.).* ☎ *212/864-5400. www.symphonyspace.org. Tickets $25–$40. Subway: 1/2/3 to 96th St.*

★ Town Hall MIDTOWN WEST

A National Historic Site, this space with outstanding acoustics has hosted performers ranging from Judy Collins to Ornette Coleman, the Klezmatics to flamenco singers. *123 W. 43rd St. (btw. Sixth & Seventh aves.).* ☎ *212/840-2824. www.the-townhall-nyc.org. Tickets $24–$150. Subway: N/Q/R/S/W/1/2/3/7 to 42nd St./Times Sq.; B/D/F/M to 42nd St.*

Live Music

Arlene's Grocery LOWER EAST SIDE A casual rock music club with a good sound system; great bang for the buck. *95 Stanton St. (btw. Ludlow & Orchard sts.).* ☎ *212/358-1633. www.arlenes grocery.net. $8–$10 cover; no cover Mon. Subway: F to Second Ave.*

★ **B. B. King Blues Club & Grill** THEATER DISTRICT This 550-seat venue plays the blues (naturally) as well as pop, funk, and country. A Beatles-tribute brunch is held on Saturdays, a gospel brunch on Sundays. *237 W. 42nd St. (btw. Seventh & Eighth aves.).* ☎ *212/997-4144. www.bbkingblues. com. Tickets $15–$100. Subway: A/C/E/Q/W/1/2/3/7/to 42nd St.*

★★ **Birdland** MIDTOWN WEST A legendary jazz club and one of the city's favorites. *315 W. 44th St. (btw. Eighth & Ninth aves.).* ☎ *212/ 581-3080. www.birdlandjazz.com. Tickets $10–$40. Subway: A/C/E to 42nd St.*

★ **Blue Note** GREENWICH VILLAGE Cool-jazz fans take note: This Village spot has an excellent sound system and sightlines. *131 W. 3rd St. (at Sixth Ave.).*

Radio City Music Hall.

☎ *212/475-8592. www.bluenote. net. Tickets $20–$55. Subway: A/B/ C/D/E/F/M to W. 4th St.*

★★ **Bowery Ballroom** LOWER EAST SIDE Another Art Deco wonder—this one with a big stage and good sightlines from every corner. Such alt-rockers as Kurt Vile perform here, as do stalwarts like Emmylou Harris. *6 Delancey St. (at Bowery).* ☎ *212/533-2111. www. boweryballroom.com. Tickets $13– $40. Subway: F/J/M/Z to Delancey St.*

★ **Café Carlyle** UPPER EAST SIDE This classic cabaret lounge was once the domain of the late Bobby Short. Now it's the venue for a rotating lineup of musical stars; Woody Allen and his New Orleans–style jazz band perform often. *Carlyle Hotel, 35 E. 76th St.* ☎ *212/ 744-1600. www.thecarlyle.com. Tickets $55–$170. Subway: 6 to 77th St.*

★ **Iridium** THEATER DISTRICT Guitar great Les Paul performed at this glamorous jazz club regularly before he passed away in 2009. Today, the club's Les Paul Guitar Tributes are held every Monday. The Iridium also hosts tributes to such jazz greats as Thelonious Monk and Charles Mingus. *1650 Broadway (at 51st St.).* ☎ *212/582-2121. www.iridiumjazzclub.com. Tickets $31–$50. Subway: 1 to 50th St.*

Irving Plaza GRAMERCY PARK This midsize music hall remains a prime stop for such rock bands as the Black Crowes and the B-52s. *17 Irving Place (at 15th St.).* ☎ *212/777-1224. www.irvingplaza. com. Tickets $20–$55. Subway: L/N/R/4/5/6 to 14th St./Union Sq.*

★★ **Jazz Standard** MURRAY HILL One of the city's largest jazz clubs, Jazz Standard has a retro vibe and the best food of any club. (It's part of, and downstairs from,

Birdland jazz.

Blue Smoke, a barbecue joint.) *116 E. 27th St. (btw. Park Ave. S. & Lexington Ave.).* ☎ *212/576-2232. www.jazzstandard.net. $20–$35 cover. Subway: 6 to 28th St.*

Joe's Pub EAST VILLAGE Located in the Public Theater and named for its founder, Joseph Papp, this eclectic supper club is always full of pleasant musical surprises. *425 Lafayette St. (btw. Astor Place & E. 4th St.).* ☎ *212/539-8778. www.joespub.com. Subway: 6 to Astor Place.*

★★ Mercury Lounge LOWER EAST SIDE The ideal live-music rock-'n'-roll bar. *217 E. Houston St. (btw. Essex & Ludlow sts.).* ☎ *212/260-4700. www.mercury loungenyc.com. $10–$12 cover; some shows require tickets. Subway: F to Second Ave.*

★★ Metropolitan Room FLAT-IRON DISTRICT This sexy spot gets raves as one of the best cabarets and concert venues in town. *34 W. 22nd St. (btw. Fifth & Sixth aves.).* ☎ *212/206-0440. www.metropolitan room.com. $15–$35 cover; 2-drink minimum. Subway: N/R to 23rd St.*

★ Paris Blues HARLEM An old-school pass-the-hat jazz joint where the music cooks into the wee hours. A two-drink minimum will get you a night's worth of music from R&B to reggae. But maybe even more entertaining than the music is the local cast of characters that gives Paris Blues that old-time Harlem feel. No fancy stuff here—just raw, good-time funky fun. *2012 Adam Clayton Powell, Jr., Blvd. (at W. 121st St).* ☎ *212/864-9110. www.paris-bluesharlem.com. Subway: 2/3 to 125th St.*

Broadway Theaters

In the Big Apple, you'll find a kaleidoscopic mix of big-budget blockbusters and alternative, experimental shows. Broadway is the place to see glorious spectacles like *Wicked*, classics like *12 Angry Men*, and first-run hits like *The Nance*. Casts often include faces you'll recognize from the big screen—Kevin Spacey, Patrick Stewart, and Glenn Close, to name a few. And these days, even the smaller and alternative shows are frequently lit by star power (Tim Robbins's Actors' Gang are regulars at the Public Theater; p 143). For information on tickets, see "Getting Broadway Tickets" (p 147); for a list of theaters, see p 148 or the map on p 129.

Lincoln Center for the Performing Arts.

★★ **Smalls** GREENWICH VIL-LAGE *New York* magazine calls this intimate club "the quintessential jazz dive," and it's a holy hang-out for jazz aficionados who don't mind the subterranean space and unforgiving wooden chairs. *183 W. 10th St. (btw. Seventh Ave. S. & W. 4th St.).* ☎ *212/252-5091. www. smallsjazzclub.com. $20 cover ($10 after 1am). Subway: A/B/C/D/E/F/M to W. 4th St.*

★★ **Smoke** UPPER WEST SIDE . Going strong for almost 14 years—and even despite expanding and adding a supper club— Smoke still hasn't forgotten its initial objective of offering intimate, familiar, reliable jazz. Such mainstays as Mike LeDonne, John Farnsworth, and Eric Alexander, who helped launch Smoke, still make it their home with regular gigs. *2751*

The Ambassador Theater on Broadway.

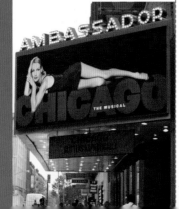

Broadway (btw. 105th & 106th sts.). ☎ *212/864-6662. www.smokejazz. com. $35 cover Fri–Sat. Subway: 1 to 103rd St.*

★★ **S.O.B.'s** SOHO This top world-music venue features Brazilian, Caribbean, and Latin beats. The music is so hot that you won't be able to stay in your seat. *204 Varick St. (at W. Houston St.).* ☎ *212/243-4940. www.sobs.com. $10–$32 cover. Subway: 1 to Houston St.*

The Village Vanguard GREEN-WICH VILLAGE Since 1935, this club has been showcasing jazz artists. Many of the greats, including Sonny Rollins and John Coltrane, have recorded live jazz albums here. *178 Seventh Ave. S. (just below 11th St.).* ☎ *212/255-4037. www. villagevanguard.com. Tickets $20–$25; 1-drink minimum. Subway: 1/2/3 to 14th St.*

Opera

★★★ **Metropolitan Opera** LINCOLN CENTER Opera aficionados consider this one of the most electrifying companies in the world. *At the Metropolitan Opera House, Lincoln Center, Broadway & 64th St.* ☎ *212/362-6000. www.metopera family.org. Tickets $17–$295. Subway: 1 to 66th St.*

★ **New York City Opera** LIN-COLN CENTER NYC Opera's repertoire includes more modern and experimental works than the Met's

Getting Broadway Tickets

If your heart is set on seeing a particular show, buy tickets in advance from **TeleCharge** (☎ 212/239-6200; www.telecharge.com) or **Ticketmaster** (☎ 212/307-4100; www.ticketmaster.com). Or save up to 50 percent on tickets through the free membership programs at **www.broadwaybox.com**, **www.broadway.com**, **www.playbill.com**, or **www.theatermania.com**. **Same-day tickets** for many top Broadway, off-Broadway, and Lincoln Center shows can be bought in person at the **TKTS booth** (☎ 212/912-9770; www.tdf.org) in Times Square on the pedestrian island called Duffy Square at 47th Street and Broadway (for evening performances, get to TKTS on Mon & Wed–Sat 3–8pm, Tues 2–8pm, and Sun 3pm to half-hour before curtain time; for matinees, be at TKTS on Wed and Sat 10am–2pm, and Sun 11am–3pm). No evening tickets are sold from 10am to 2pm at Times Square. As of press time, the **South Street Seaport TKTS booth** (199 Water St.) was still closed due to damage from Hurricane Sandy. A TKTS booth has opened in **Downtown Brooklyn** (1 MetroTech Center, at Jay St. & Myrtle Ave.; Tues–Sat 11am–6pm). Most tickets are sold at half-price, although some are discounted only 25 percent. A $4 TKTS service charge is added.

(above), but the singers are less well known. *At the New York State Theater, Lincoln Center, Broadway & 64th St.* ☎ 212/870-5570. www.nycopera.com. Tickets $12–$140. Subway: 1 to 66th St.

★ **New York Gilbert & Sullivan Players** MIDTOWN   Lighthearted operetta is the ticket here, and no one does it better. The troupe performs at Symphony Space (p 143). *Symphony Space, 2537 Broadway (at 95th St.).* ☎ 212/864-5400. www.nygasp.org. Tickets $49–$82. Subway: 1/2/3 to 96th St.

Stand-up Comedy
★★ **Carolines on Broadway** THEATER DISTRICT   Hot headliners come to this upscale club—Jerry Seinfeld, Joel McHale, and Patton Oswalt have all taken the stage. *1626 Broadway (btw. 49th & 50th sts.).* ☎ 212/757-4100. www.

carolines.com. $15–$49 cover. Subway: N/R to 49th St.; 1 to 50th St.

★ **Comedy Cellar** GREENWICH VILLAGE   This intimate subterranean club is a favorite among comedy cognoscenti. It gets names you'd expect (Dave Chappelle, Chris Rock) and a few you wouldn't (William Shatner). *117 Macdougal St. (btw. Minetta Lane & W. 3rd St.).* ☎ 212/254-3480. www.comedycellar.com. $10–$24 cover. Subway: A/B/C/D/E/F/M/S to W. 4th St.

★ **Gotham Comedy Club** FLATIRON DISTRICT   Big names are frequently on the marquee in this large, 1920s-era space next door to the Chelsea Hotel. The "New Talent Showcase" is a staple. *208 W. 23rd St. (btw. Seventh & Eighth aves.).* ☎ 212/367-9000. www.gothamcomedyclub.com. $12–$30 cover. Subway: F/N/R to 23rd St.

Broadway **Theaters**

Al Hirschfeld. 302 W. 45th St. ☎ 212/560-2163.

Ambassador. 219 W. 49th St. ☎ 212/239-6200.

American Airlines. 227 W. 42nd St. ☎ 212/719-1300.

August Wilson. 245 W. 52nd St. ☎ 212/239-6200.

Belasco. 111 W. 44th St. ☎ 212/239-6200.

Bernard B. Jacobs. 242 W. 45th St. ☎ 212/239-6200.

Samuel J. Friedman 261 W. 47th St. ☎ 212/239-6222.

Booth. 222 W. 45th St. ☎ 888/847-4869.

Broadhurst. 235 W. 44th St. ☎ 212/239-6200.

Broadway. 1681 Broadway. ☎ 212/239-6200.

Brooks Atkinson. 256 W. 47th St. ☎ 212/719-4099.

Circle in the Square. 1633 Broadway. ☎ 212/307-0388.

Cort. 138 W. 48th St. ☎ 212/239-6200.

Ethel Barrymore. 243 W. 47th St. ☎ 212/239-6200.

Eugene O'Neill. 230 W. 49th St. ☎ 212/840-8181.

Foxwoods. 213 W. 42nd St. ☎ 212/556-4750.

Gershwin. 222 W. 51st St. ☎ 212/586-6510.

Helen Hayes. 240 W. 44th St. ☎ 212/944-9450.

Imperial. 249 W. 45th St. ☎ 212/239-6200.

John Golden. 252 W. 45th St. ☎ 212/560-2164.

Longacre. 220 W. 48th St. ☎ 212/239-6200.

Lunt-Fontanne. 205 W. 46th St. ☎ 212/575-9200.

Lyceum. 149 W. 45th St. ☎ 212/239-6200.

Majestic. 245 W. 44th St. ☎ 212/239-6215.

Marquis. 1535 Broadway. ☎ 212/382-0100.

Minskoff. 200 W. 45th St. ☎ 212/869-0550.

Music Box. 239 W. 45th St. ☎ 212/560-2165.

Nederlander. 208 W. 41st St. ☎ 212/921-8000.

Neil Simon. 250 W. 52nd St. ☎ 212/757-8646.

New Amsterdam. 214 W. 42nd St. ☎ 212/282-2900.

New Victory. 209 W. 42nd St. ☎ 646/223-3020.

Palace. 1564 Broadway. ☎ 212/730-8200.

Gerald Schoenfeld. 236 W. 45th St. ☎ 212/239-6200.

Richard Rodgers. 226 W. 46th St. ☎ 212/221-1211.

St. James. 246 W. 44th St. ☎ 212/239-6200.

Shubert. 225 W. 44th St. ☎ 212/239-6200.

Studio 54. 254 W. 54th St. ☎ 212/719-1300.

Vivian Beaumont. 150 W. 65th St. ☎ 212/362-7600.

Walter Kerr. 219 W. 48th St. ☎ 212/239-6200.

Winter Garden. 1634 Broadway. ☎ 212/239-6200. ●

Hotel Best Bets

Most Romantic
Inn at Irving Place $$$ 56 Irving Place (p 157)

Hotel with the Best Restaurant and Bar
Gramercy Park Hotel $$$$ 2 Lexington Ave. (p 156)

Best Boutique Hotel
Crosby Street Hotel $$$ 79 Crosby St. (p 155); Hotel Giraffe $$ 365 Park Ave. S. (p 156)

Best Old-School Glamour
The Carlyle $$$$ 35 E. 76th St. (p 155)

Best Hidden Gem
Gild Hall $$ 15 Gold St. (p 156)

Most Luxurious Hotel
The Peninsula—New York $$$$ 700 Fifth Ave. (p 160)

Best Budget Hotel
La Quinta Inn $ 17 W. 32nd St. (p 158)

Best for Kids
Hotel Beacon $$$$ 230 Broadway (p 156)

Best Value
Casablanca Hotel $$–$$$ 147 W. 43rd St. (p 155)

Best Service
Ritz Carlton Central Park, New York $$$$ 50 Central Park South (p 160)

Best Hotel in the Middle of Everything
The London NYC, $$$ 151 W. 54th St. (p 159)

Best Theme Hotel
The Library Hotel $$$ 299 Madison Ave. (p 159)

Most Charming B&B
The Inn on 23rd $$ 131 W. 23rd St. (p 157)

Best for Celebrity Sightings
The Mercer $$$ 147 Mercer St. (p 159)

Best Views
Ritz-Carlton New York $$$ 2 West St. (p 160); and Ink 48 $$–$$$ 653 11th Ave. (p 157)

Best Hotel Pool
Greenwich Hotel, $$$ 377 Greenwich St. (p 156)

Best for Business Travelers
Wall Street Inn $$ 9 S. William St. (p 161); and The Benjamin $$$ 125 E. 50th St. (p 154)

Previous page: The funky lobby of the Crosby Street Hotel.

Downtown Hotels

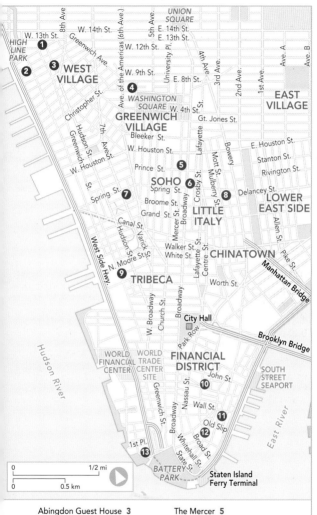

Abingdon Guest House **3**

Andaz Wall Street **11**

Crosby Street Hotel **6**

Gild Hall **10**

The Greenwich Hotel **9**

The Gansevoort **1**

The Jane **2**

The Mercer **5**

The Nolitan **8**

Ritz-Carlton New York,
   Battery Park **13**

Trump SoHo **7**

Wall Street Inn **12**

Washington Square Hotel **4**

The Best Hotels

Midtown & Uptown Hotels

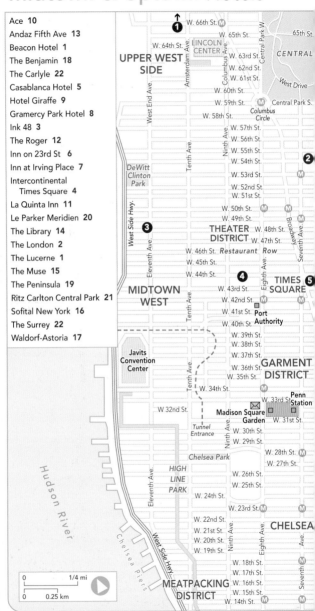

Hotels A to Z

A little bit country, a little bit rock 'n' roll: the Ace Hotel.

Abingdon Guest House WEST VILLAGE   This nine-room B&B is tucked away in two 19th-century town houses just blocks from Hudson River Park and the High Line (p 44). Oriental rugs, exposed brick, and elegant furnishings make this a romantic hideaway. *21 Eighth Ave. (btw. Jane & 12th sts.).* ☎ *212/243-5384. www.abingdonguesthouse. com. 9 units. Suites $169–$269. AE, DC, DISC, MC, V. Subway: A/C/E/1/2/3 to 14th St.*

★★ **Ace Hotel** FLATIRON DISTRICT   Ultrahip but attitude-free, this Pacific Coast transplant has some of the coolest amenities in town: Gibson guitars and turntables in rooms! Pembleton wool blankets on beds! Google Chrome laptops for use or purchase! Mini-Heineken kegs in full-size fridges! On top of that, there's a room for every budget (the cheapest option is bunk beds). Has a warm, buzzing lobby and a hot restaurant (**the Breslin;**

p 117). *20 W. 29th St. (btw. Fifth Ave. & Broadway).* ☎ *212/678-2222. www.acehotel.com/newyork. 273 units. Double $199–$799. AE, DISC, MC, V. Subway: N/R to 28th St.*

★★ **Andaz Fifth Avenue** MIDTOWN   Behind a nameless facade lies one of the city's smartest new hotels. The striking interior of this historic 1916 building has become a thoughtful homage to the city, with tall, factory-style shutters and edgy artwork. Rooms have extravagantly high ceilings, rainfall shower heads, and soaking tubs. Some have spectacular views of the New York Public Library, across the street. *485 Fifth Ave. (at 41st St.).* ☎ *212/601-1233. www. newyork.5thavenue.andaz.hyatt.com. 184 units. Double from $325, suite from $645. AE, DISC, MC, V. Subway: 4/5/6 to Grand Central and B/D/F to Bryant Park/42nd St.*

★★★ **Andaz Wall Street** WALL STREET   The dazzling lobby, bar, and restaurant were designed by David Rockwell, but the warm welcome is all Andaz. So what if the minimalist rooms lack the sparkle of the public spaces? The high ceilings and oak floors give the rooms a solid, grounded feel. Plus, you gotta love the complimentary Wi-Fi and minibar (sans alcohol). *75 Wall St. (at Water St.).* ☎ *212/590-1234. www.newyork.wallstreet.andaz.hyatt. com. 253 units. Double $250–$495. AE, DISC, MC, V. Subway: 2/3 to Wall St./William St. or 4/5 to Wall St.*

★★ **The Benjamin** MIDTOWN EAST   Set in a 1927 landmark building, the Benjamin combines solid bones with top-flight service and amenities. You will be supremely comfortable here. *125 E. 50th St. (at Lexington Ave.).*

☎ 212/715-2500. www.thebenjamin.
com. 209 units. Double from $459,
suite from $559. AE, DC, DISC, MC,
V. Subway: 6 to 51st St.; E/F to Lexington Ave.

★★★ The Carlyle UPPER EAST
SIDE   The old-school glamour in
this 1930 white-glove landmark is
tasteful, understated, never over-
the-top. But baby, it's plenty luxe,
all gleaming marble and custom
fabrics. **Bemelman's Bar** is a jewel.
35 E. 76th St. (at Madison Ave.).
☎ 212/744-1600. www.rosewood
hotels.com/thecarlyle. 188 units.
Double $650–$950, suite from $950.
AE, DC, DISC, MC, V. Subway: 6 to
51st St.; E/F to Lexington Ave.

★★ Casablanca Hotel MID-
TOWN WEST   An oasis in the middle of the Times Square mayhem,
the Casablanca is one of the best
moderate options in the area.
Rooms are good-size for the price,
and a homey lounge with fireplace
where daily complimentary wine
and cheese and breakfast are
served add to the value. Book
early—the word is out on the Casablanca. 147 W.43rd St. (btw. Broadway & Sixth Ave). ☎ 212/869-1212.
www.casablancahotel.com. 48 units.

Double $250–$500. AE, DC, MC, V.
Subway: N,R,Q, 1,2,3 to Times
Square–42nd St.

★★ Crosby Street Hotel
SOHO   Finding a hotel this light
and irresistibly playful in the long,
dark shadows of Crosby Street is a
revelation. Spacious rooms are
done in muted hues—mauve, plum,
apple—with plumped linens and
textured fabrics. It's elegant and
whimsical all at once.79 Crosby St.
(btw. Prince & Spring sts.).
☎ 212/226-6400. http://crosby
streethotel.com. 86 units. Double
$495–$715, suite $815–$2,250. AE,
DC, MC, V. Subway: N/R to Prince
St.; 6 to Spring St.

★ The Gansevoort MEATPACK-
ING DISTRICT   This stylish spot
has transcended its annoying initial
trendiness and established itself as
a reliable choice for service and
comfort. It has spacious rooms, a
full-service spa, and a rooftop pool.
Plunge, the rooftop bar, has
360-degree views. 18 Ninth Ave. (at
13th St.). ☎ 877/426-7386. www.
hotelgansevoort.com. 187 units. Double $295–$725, duplex penthouse
$5,000. AE, MC, V. Subway: A/C/E to
14th St.

The lobby of the Andaz Wall Street.

The Gansevoort, in the Meatpacking District.

★★ Gild Hall FINANCIAL DIS-
TRICT   This little gem is tucked away in the folds of Gold Street. The pub and restaurant are right out of a Dutch Colonial painting, with rustic wood panels, period murals, and a candlelit patina. The masculine rooms upstairs—with state-of-the-art amenities, flannel throws, and walls hung with Slim Aarons's iconic photographs—are totally 21st century, though. *15 Gold St. (at Platt St.).* ☎ *212/232-7700. www.thompsonhotels.com. 126 units. Double $237–$499, Thompson Suite $1,200. AE, MC, V. Subway: 2/3 to Fulton St.*

★★ Gramercy Park Hotel
GRAMERCY PARK   This 1925-built legend was totally redone less than a decade ago, expanding the rooms and adding 21st-century technology and elegance. Many of the large rooms have views of charming Gramercy Park, and all feature velvet upholstered beds, leather-topped tables, and photos by world famous photojournalists. Public spaces include the fabulous Rose Bar and Danny Meyer's Italian gem, Maialino. *2 Lexington Ave. (at 21st St.).* ☎ *212/920-3300. www.gramercyparkhotel.com. 185 units. Double $400–$700. AE, DC, MC, V. Subway: 6 to 23rd St.*

★★★ The Greenwich Hotel
TRIBECA   No detail or expense has been spared at this beautiful small luxury hotel (whose owners include Robert De Niro), where even the bricks are handcrafted. It's meant to feel like an 88-room home—if home is a rustically elegant country manor filled with art and antiques. It's everything a hip, edgy downtown hotel isn't—and that makes it plenty hip. *377 Greenwich St. (at N. Moore St.).* ☎ *212/941-8900. www.greenwichhotelny.com. 88 units. Double $495–$725, suite $995–$1,750. AE, DC, DISC, MC, V. Subway: 1 to Franklin St.*

★ Hotel Beacon UPPER WEST
SIDE   This solid, family-friendly choice is a short walk from **Central Park** (p 104) and the **American Museum of Natural History** (p 54). The good-value perks include large rooms with kitchenettes. *230 Broadway (at 75th St.).* ☎ *800/572-4969. www.beaconhotel.com. 260 units. Double $205, suite $255 & up. AE, DC, MC, V. Subway: 1/2/3 to 72th St.*

★★ Hotel Giraffe FLATIRON
DISTRICT   This boutique property never fails to impress. Book early to snag one of the stylish, elegant

The bar at Gild Hall.

guest rooms graced with high ceilings, velveteen upholstered chairs, and a soothing slate-gray palette. Deluxe rooms have small balconies. *365 Park Ave. S. (at 26th St.).* ☎ *212/685-7700. www.hotel giraffe.com. 72 units. Double $360–$500 w/ breakfast. AE, DC, MC, V. Subway: 6 to 28th St.*

Ink 48 MIDTOWN WEST This Kimpton-run hotel is just 1 block from the Hudson River, and although it's a bit of a trek from Times Square and the closest subway, the western views from the hotel room's floor-to-ceiling windows of New Jersey and the nearby U.S.S. *Intrepid*, and those facing east and the spires of Midtown, are some of the best in the city. *653 11th Ave. (at 48th St.)* ☎ *212/757-0088. www.ink48.com. 222 units. Double $350–$450. AE, DC, MC, V. Subway: C, E to 50th Street.*

★ The Roger MURRAY HILL This under-the-radar boutique hotel on Madison Avenue manages to be both hip (flatscreen TVs, iPod docking stations) and comfy (quilts on plump beds), with a buzzing mezzanine lounge. *131 Madison Ave. (at 31st St.).* ☎ *888/448-7788. www.hotelroger williams.com. 193 units. Double $365–$535. AE, DC, DISC, MC, V. Subway: 6 to 28th St.*

★★ Inn at Irving Place GRAMERCY Bored with sleek minimalism? This 170-year-old town house marries 19th-century elegance with 21st-century luxe (antique beds plumped up with Frette linens). Spacious rooms have antiques and art, nonworking fireplaces, and big bathrooms. *56 Irving Place (btw. 17th & 18th sts.).* ☎ *800/685-1447. www.innatirving. com. 12 units. Double $445–$645. AE, DC, MC, V. Subway: N/R/4/5/6 to 14th St./Union Sq.*

The discreet Inn at Irving Place.

★★ The Inn on 23rd CHELSEA There's nothing frou-frou about this handsome "urban B&B," one of Manhattan's few full-service B&Bs. Each spacious guest room has been decorated with a personal touch. Kids are welcome. *131 W. 23rd St. (btw. Sixth & Seventh aves.).* ☎ *212/463-0330. www.innon23rd. com. 14 units. Double $175–$250. AE, MC, V. Subway: F/1/ to 23rd St.*

★★ InterContinental New York Times Square THEATER DISTRICT The wall-length fire pit in the lobby is a warm welcome on a brisk night. Opened in 2010, this 607-room hotel has a smart location that's tucked away from the Times Square hordes. The big, handsome rooms are done in creamy champagne hues; look for such luxe touches as walk-in rain showers and hand-blown bathroom glasses. Tower Avenue studios come with five-corner views. *300 W. 44th St. (at Eighth Ave.).* ☎ *888/424-6835. www.ihg.com. 607 units. Double $315–$630. AE, MC, V. Subway: A/C/E/1/2/3 to Times Sq.*

★ The Jane WEST VILLAGE Two-thirds of the units in this "micro hotel" are 50-square-foot spaces complete with bed (or bunk bed),

A cabin room at the Jane.

flatscreen TV, Wi-Fi, A/C, and shared bathrooms—all yours for $99 a night. But with such fabulous public spaces—a massive lobby bar with fireplace, a rooftop lounge overlooking the Hudson River— who needs a big, pricey room to rattle around in? *113 Jane St. (at the West Side Hwy.).* ☎ *212/924-6700. www.thejanenyc.com. 210 units. Room $99–$250. AE, MC, V. Subway: A/C/E to 14th St.*

★ **La Quinta Inn** MIDTOWN WEST   The location in the heart of Koreatown (with good Korean BBQs and karaoke bars up and

The lobby of Le Parker-Meridien.

down the street) is 2 blocks from the **Empire State Building** (p 6) and **Macy's** (p 95). The spacious if style-free rooms have amenities you wouldn't expect from a moderate- priced hotel, such as free Wi-Fi. Or you can enjoy the fresh air at the rooftop bar instead. *17 W. 32nd St. (btw. Fifth Ave. & Broadway).* ☎ *800/567-7720. www.applecore hotels.com or www.lq. com. 182 units. Double $215 & up. AE, DC, DISC, MC, V. Subway: B/D/F/M/N/R to 34th St.*

★★ **Le Parker-Meridien** TIMES SQUARE   The lobby's soaring atrium puts you squarely in a New York state of mind; it's a bustling spot, with a sexy Moroccan-style lobby bar **(the Knave)** in one corner and a roadhouse burger spot **(Burger Joint**—which makes one of the best burgers in the city) tucked in another. This 42-floor hotel has just refreshed its rooms in olive, orange, and brown hues, and they're looking spiffy indeed. Cheeky, too: The hotel's "DO NOT DIS- TURB" signs read "FUHGEDDABOUDIT." The rooftop pool has Central Park views. *119 W. 56th St. (btw. Sixth & Seventh aves.).* ☎ *212/245-5000. www.parkermeridien.com. 725 units. Double $600–$800, suite $780 & up.*

AE, DC, DISC, MC, V. Subway: B/D/E to Seventh Ave.

★ **The Library Hotel** MIDTOWN EAST Each of the 10 floors here is dedicated to a major category of the Dewey Decimal System. Rooms have a Deco elegance, done in buttery yellow and loaded with books to read. The Petite Rooms are a solid value. The **Writer's Den,** on the 14th floor, has the dog-eared feel of a beloved book. *299 Madison Ave. (at 41st St.). ☎ 212/983-4500. www.libraryhotel.com. 60 units. Double $260–$500. AE, DC, MC, V. Subway: 4/5/6/7/S to 42nd St.*

★★ **The London** MIDTOWN WEST In the heart of Midtown, the sleek and fashionable London has plenty to offer, including, most important, spacious rooms with spectacular city views. Suites feature separate parlors, some with French doors. Fine dining at Gordon Ramsay at the London as well as Maze by Gordon Ramsay add to the hotel's allure. *151 W. 54th St (btw. Sixth & Seventh aves.). ☎ 866/690-2029. www.thelondonnyc.com. 562 units. Double $400–$800. AE, DC, MC, V. Subway: B, D, E to Seventh Ave.*

The Lucerne UPPER WEST SIDE The location close to Central Park, the Museum of Natural History, and all the charm of the Upper West Side make this hotel, housed in a classic Beaux Arts building, an outstanding moderate choice. The service is impeccable, and rooms are well equipped and big enough for kings, queens, or two doubles. Suites have kitchenettes, making it a good choice for families. Some rooms even have views of the Hudson River. *201 W. 79th St. (at Amsterdam Ave.). ☎ 212/875-1000. www.thelucernehotel.com. 200 units. Double $250–$600. AE, DC, DISC, MC, V. Subway: 1 to 79th St.*

★★ **The Mercer** SOHO Ignore the revolving door of celebs and thrill to the high-ceilinged rooms, lush linens, and big marble bathrooms. The Mercer remains one of the standard-bearers of downtown style. *147 Mercer St. (at Prince St.). ☎ 888/918-6060. www.mercerhotel.com. 75 units. Double $525–$950. AE, DC, DISC, MC, V. Subway: N/R to Prince St.*

★ **The Muse** TIMES SQUARE If anything in the middle of Times Square can be called an oasis of calm, this is it. This chic Kimpton property has stylishly renovated rooms (some with balconies) and loads of top-drawer amenities. The Muse plays host to the NYPD on New Year's Eve. *139 W. 46th St. (btw. Broadway & Sixth Ave.). ☎ 877/692-6873. www.themusehotel.com. 200 units. Double $230–$400. AE, DC, DISC, MC, V. Subway: A/C/E/1/2/3 to Times Sq.*

★ **The Nolitan** NOLITA Located close to Chinatown, Little Italy, Soho, and Nolita, the Nolitan fits in snugly with those unique neighborhoods. This boutique charmer features cozy rooms, many with balconies, all with open views from

The Peninsula.

The Ritz-Carlton, as seen from New York Harbor.

oversize windows. The hotel even offers free bike rentals to better explore the downtown neighborhoods. *30 Kenmare St. (btw. Elizabeth & Mott sts.).* ☎ *212/925-2556. www.nolitanhotel.com. 55 units. Double $300–$500. AE, DC, MC, V. Subway: 6 to Spring St.*

★★★ The Peninsula—New York MIDTOWN

A dream of a hotel, almost perfect in every way. Housed in a 1905 landmark building, the Peninsula has some of the most tastefully luxurious (and priciest) rooms in town. Take the curving stairway up from the world-class spa to the 22nd-floor heated pool, with Central Park and Fifth Avenue views. *700 Fifth Ave. (at 55th St.).* ☎ *800/262-9467. www.peninsula. com. 239 units. Double $975–$1,175, suite $1,375–$16,000. AE, DC, DISC, MC, V. Subway: E/F to Fifth Ave.*

★★★ kids Ritz-Carlton New York, Battery Park BATTERY

PARK Newly renovated guest rooms offer luxurious comfort and a family-friendly welcome. **Statue of Liberty** (p 17) rooms have magnificent views of New York Harbor and telescopes to zoom in on the beauteous Lady Liberty. Upgrade to a Club Level room for daylong perks in the Club Lounge, such as complimentary food and drinks. *2 West St. (at 1st Place).* ☎ *800/241-3333. www.ritzcarlton.com. 298 units. Double $425–$545, suite $545–$1,395. AE, DC, DISC, MC, V. Subway: 4/5 to Bowling Green.*

★★★ kids Ritz-Carlton Central Park, New York MIDTOWN

WEST Without an intimidating overabundance of style, this Ritz-Carlton, facing Central Park, maintains an homey elegance that is rare in a hotel of this category. Extremely kid-friendly, suites have sofa beds and can accommodate cribs or rollaway beds. Children are given in-room milk and cookies, while adults can luxuriate at the hotel's La Prairie spa. *50 Central Park South (at Sixth Ave).* ☎ *212/308-9100. www.ritzcarlton.com. 259 units. Double $700–$900. AE, DC, MC, V. Subway: N, R to Fifth Ave.*

★ Sofitel New York MIDTOWN

WEST Built in 2000, the 30-story Sofitel has an elegant, marbled lobby with a Deco-style restaurant and bar. Rooms are standard but spacious and soundproofed. *45 W.*

The lounge of the Sofitel.

Money-Saving Tips on Lodging

New York is one of the most expensive cities in the country—a fact you'll comprehend when you try to book a hotel. To get the best price, consider these tips. **Schedule in the off season and at off times:** Hotels charge premium rates around the Christmas holidays, for example, and prices climb sky-high during major events, such as the NYC Marathon. Rates at business hotels often drop on weekends, however, when rooms empty out. **Look for off-the-beaten-path locations:** A number of big chains, such as Hampton Inn and Ramada Inn, offer all-suite offshoots in safe but less touristy neighborhoods. The suites provide an extra bonus: self-catering capabilities to save on meals. **Check hotel websites** for exclusive online deals. **Consider pods**—pod-style hotels, that is, offering tiny rail-inspired rooms packed with amenities—like downtown's **The Jane** (p 156) and the **Pod Hotel** (230 E. 51st St., at Third Ave.; ☎ 212/355-0300; www.thepodhotel.com). So what if your room is miniscule? You'll be too busy to spend much time there anyway.

44th St. (btw. Fifth & Sixth aves.). ☎ 212/354-8844. www.sofitel.com. 398 units. Double $494–$666. AE, DC, MC, V. Subway: B/D/F/M to 42nd St.

The Surrey UPPER EAST SIDE An enviable Museum Mile location just adds to the allure of the Surrey, which was renovated a few years back and now melds its classic Art Deco roots with contemporary art. Rooms vary in size from spacious suites to standard, although well equipped, rooms. What really sets the Surrey apart are the extras, such as a rooftop garden, a Cornelia spa, and room service from the acclaimed Café Boulud. 20 E. 76th St. (at Madison Ave.). ☎ 212/288-3700. 189 units. Double $450–$575. AE, DC, DISC, MC, V. Subway: 6 to 77th St.

★★ Trump SoHo SOHO This sleek 46-floor tower hotel opened in 2010 in a nondescript commercial neighborhood near the entrance to the Holland Tunnel. But inside all is pampering and serenity. Rooms are artfully designed, with big Turkish-marble bathrooms. And those views! It's a wide-open Hudson River panorama. 246 Spring St. (at Varick St.). ☎ 212/842-5500 . www.trumphotelcollection/soho.com. 391 units. Double $599–$659, suite $799–$859. AE, DISC, MC, V. Subway: 6 to Spring St.

★ Waldorf=Astoria MIDTOWN EAST This massive Art Deco masterpiece is a genuine New York landmark. The 1,000-plus rooms mean the pace can be hectic, but rates are competitive. 301 Park Ave. (btw. 49th & 50th sts.). ☎ 212/355-3000. www.waldorfastoria.com. 1,245 units. Double $320–$400, suite $420–$740. AE, DC, DISC, MC, V. Subway: 6 to 51st St.

★ The Wall Street Inn FINANCIAL DISTRICT This intimate, seven-story Lower Manhattan oasis is warm, comforting, and serene.

B&Bs & Apartment Stays

Yes, hotel prices are high in New York, and the costs climb even higher for families paying for extra people in the room. Oh, and did we mention hotel room taxes? (Tack on 14.25 percent to your total bill.) Save big bucks, enjoy more room, and live among the locals by staying in a B&B. Alas, short-term apartment rentals are now illegal, but the city has plenty of reliable operators for stays of a month or more. These well-established, expert brokers offer a range of lodgings, from elegant rooms in prewar apartment buildings to sunny, fully furnished apartments in historic brownstones. Fully equipped kitchens help you save big on meals. Prices can start as low as $90 a night. Check out **NY Habitat** (www.nyhabitat. com; $115–$300/night based on a 3-night stay, with weekly and monthly rates available) for furnished apartments; **City Sonnet** (www.citysonnet.com; $95–$700 double) for both hosted and unhosted lodging in apartments and artists' lofts; or **Manhattan Getaways** (www.manhattangetaways.com; $125–$165 room, $1,650–$1,750 apt.) for furnished rooms or private apartments. **Airbnb** (www.airbnb.com) can connect you with New Yorkers who want to rent out a room in their apartments.

Friendly, professional, personalized service is the hallmark. Look for discounted weekend rates. *9 S. William St. (at Broad St.).* ☎ *212/747-1500. www.thewallstreetinn.com. 46 units. Double $159–$399. AE, DC, DISC, MC, V. Subway: 2/3 to Wall St.; 4/5 to Bowling Green.*

Washington Square Hotel
GREENWICH VILLAGE   The rooms are smallish but pleasingly outfitted in this moderately priced hotel facing Washington Square Park. It's worth paying a few extra dollars for a south-facing room on a high floor. *103 Waverly Place (btw. Fifth & Sixth aves.).* ☎ *212/777-9515. www.ws hotel.com. 150 units. Double $244–$385. AE, MC, V. Subway: A/B/C/D/E/ F/M to W. 4th St. (use 3rd St. exit).* ●

The Art Deco Washington Square Hotel.

The **Savvy Traveler**

Before You Go

Government Tourist Offices

In the U.S.: NYC & Company, 810 Seventh Ave., New York, NY 10019; ☎ 212/484-1200; www.nycgo.com. **In the U.K.:** NYCVB Visitor Information Center, 36 Southwark Bridge Rd., London, SE1 9EU; ☎ 020/7202-6368.

The Best Times to Go

July and August are hot and humid, but because the local population tries to escape, the city is far less crowded. There are plenty of free alfresco events too. December brings crowds and the highest hotel rates; January and February are relatively cheap but very chilly. But there's nothing like New York in late spring or fall when the weather is mild.

Festivals & Special Events

WINTER For information on the lighting of the **Rockefeller Center Christmas Tree,** call ☎ 212/332-6700. On **New Year's Eve, the** most famous party of them all takes place in Times Square (☎ 212/768-1560; www.timessquarenyc.org). During **Restaurant Week** (1 week in winter and 1 week in summer, and usually extended for more than just 1 week), you can enjoy $24 prix-fixe lunch menus or $35 dinner menus at some of the best restaurants in the city (☎ 212/484-1222; www.nycgo.com).

SPRING The **Pier Antiques Show,** the city's largest antiques show, takes place in March (http://stellashows.com for this and additional shows) as does, of course, the **St. Patrick's Day Parade** (http://nycstpatricksparade.org) on the 17th.

Previous page: Walking the High Line elevated park.

The **Easter Parade** (☎ 212/484-1222)—not a traditional parade, but a flamboyant fashion display along Fifth Avenue from 48th to 57th streets—is on Easter Sunday.

SUMMER All summer long, the **Lincoln Center Festival** (☎ 212/7210-6500; www.lincolncenterfestival.org) celebrates the best of the performing arts from all over the world (tickets go on sale in late May). **SummerStage** (☎ 212/360-2756; www.summerstage.org) is a summer-long festival of outdoor performances in Central Park, featuring world music, pop, folk, and jazz artists; the New York Grand Opera; and the Chinese Golden Dragon Acrobats, among others. At the same time and also in Central Park, well-known actors take on the Bard in the Public Theater's long-running **Shakespeare in the Park** series (http://shakespeareinthepark.org). The **Independence Day Harbor Festival and Fourth of July Fireworks Spectacular** (☎ 212/484-1222, or Macy's Visitor Center at 212/494-4662) takes place on July 4. Dance till you drop at **Midsummer Night Swing** (☎ 212/875-5456; http://new.lincolncenter.org/live), 3 weeks of outdoor dance parties held in Lincoln Center's Damrosch Park.

FALL The **West Indian–American Day Parade** (☎ 718/467-1797; http://wiadca.com), an annual Brooklyn event on Labor Day, is New York's best street festival. The **Greenwich Village Halloween Parade** (www.halloween-nyc.com) on October 31 is a flamboyant parade that everyone is welcome to join. Something everyone should do at least once is see the **Radio City Music Hall Christmas Spectacular** (☎ 212/247-4777 or

Ticketmaster at 212/307-1000; www.
radiocitychristmas.com/newyork)
and watch the **Macy's Thanksgiving Day Parade** (☎ 212/494-4495).

The Weather
The worst weather in New York is
during that long week or 10 days
that arrive between mid-July and
August when the temperatures soar
up to 100°F (38°C) with 90 percent
humidity. Another time when you
might not want to stroll around the
city is midwinter, when temperatures drop to around 20°F (–7°C)
and the winds whip through the
concrete canyons.

Useful Websites
- **www.nycgo.com:** A wealth of
free information about the city
- **www.nymag.com:** Terrific coverage of arts and events from
New York magazine
- **www.timeout.com/newyork:**
Full listings, restaurant reviews,
shopping, and nightlife
- **www.panynj.gov** and **www.
mta.info:** Transit info
- **www.weather.gov:** Up-to-the-
minute weather

Restaurant & Theater Reservations
We can't say it enough: Book well in
advance if you're determined to eat
at a particular spot or see a certain

show—especially if you're visiting at
a peak time. If you're determined to
eat at a hot restaurant, ask for early
or late hours—often tables are available before 6:30pm and after 9pm.
Or ask about seating at the bar,
which is often the best venue in the
house anyway.

If you're interested in a popular
show, call or go online for tickets
well before your trip. Try **TeleCharge** (☎ 212/239-6200) or **Ticketmaster** (☎ 212/307-4100; www.
ticketmaster.com). **TKTS** (p 147)
offers last-minute theater seats.

Cell Phones (Mobiles)
In general, it's a good bet that your
phone will work in New York on
either **CDMA** or **GSM wireless networks;** in fact, the largest wireless
providers (that is, Verizon, AT&T,
and T-Mobile) in the region have
upgraded their data networks to
the new higher-speed "4G" (fourth-
generation wireless) standard (available only on compatible phones).
However, foreign visitors may or
may not be able to send SMS (text
messages) overseas or receive and
send data at 4G speeds. Assume
nothing—call your wireless provider
to get the full scoop.

You can always rent a phone
from **InTouch USA** (☎ 800/872-
7626; www.intouchglobal.com), but
beware that you'll pay $1 per minute or more for airtime.

Getting **There**

By Plane
Three major airports serve New
York City: **John F. Kennedy International Airport** (☎ 718/244-4444)
in Queens is about 15 miles (24km;
1 hr. driving time) from midtown
Manhattan; **LaGuardia Airport**
(☎ 718/533-3400), also in Queens,

is about 8 miles (13km; 30 min.)
from Midtown; and **Newark International Airport** (☎ 973/961-6000)
in nearby New Jersey is about 16
miles (26km; 45 min.) from midtown. Always allow extra time,
though, especially during rush hour,
peak holiday travel times, and if

you're taking a bus. Information on all three is available online at **www.panynj.gov/airports**.

For ease and convenience, your best bet is to stay away from public transportation when traveling to and from the airport. **Taxis** are a quick and convenient alternative. They're available at designated taxi stands outside the terminals; most take credit cards. Fares, whether fixed or metered, do not include bridge and tunnel tolls ($8–$10) or a tip for the cabbie (15–20 percent is customary). They do include all passengers in the cab and luggage (from 8pm–6am, a $1 surcharge also applies on New York yellow cabs). **From JFK:** A flat rate of $52 to Manhattan (plus tolls and tip) is charged. **From LaGuardia:** $24 to $30, metered, plus tolls and tip. **From Newark:** The dispatcher for New Jersey taxis gives you a slip of paper with a flat rate ranging from $50 to $75 (toll and tip extra), depending on where you're going in Manhattan. The yellow-cab fare from Manhattan to Newark is the meter amount plus $15 and tolls (about $69–$75, perhaps a few dollars more with tip).

Private car and limousine companies provide convenient 24-hour door-to-door airport transfers. They are a little more expensive than taxis, but they're a good idea if you're traveling at rush hour because they charge flat fees. Call at least 24 hours in advance, and a driver will meet you near baggage claim. I use **Dial 7** (☎ 800/777-7777; www.dial7.com) and **Carmel** (☎ 800/922-7635 or 212/666-6666).

AirTrains ($5–$14) are available at Newark and JFK and will certainly save you money, but skip the AirTrain JFK if you have mobility issues, mountains of luggage, or small children. You'll find it easier to rely on a taxi, car service, or shuttle service that can offer you

door-to-door transfers. For information, check out **AirTrain JFK** (www.airtrainjfk.com) and **AirTrain Newark** (☎ 888/EWR-INFO; www.airtrainnewark.com). The latter works pretty well, but you will have to change trains at a NJ Transit station to get to Penn Station.

Bus and shuttle services provide a comfortable and less expensive (but usually more time-consuming) option for airport transfers than taxis and car services. The blue vans of **SuperShuttle** (☎ 800/258-3826; www.supershuttle.com) serve all three airports; fares are $15 to $22 per person. **The New York Airport Service** (☎ 718/560-3915; www.nyairportservice.com) buses travel from JFK and LaGuardia to the Port Authority Bus Terminal (42nd St. and Eighth Ave.), Grand Central Terminal (Park Ave., btw. 41st & 42nd sts.), and to select midtown hotels. One-way fares run between $12 and $15 per person.

By Car

From New Jersey and points west, there are three Hudson River crossings into the city's west side: the **Holland Tunnel** (lower Manhattan), the **Lincoln Tunnel** (Midtown), and the **George Washington Bridge** (upper Manhattan). From upstate New York, the **Tappan Zee Bridge** spans the Hudson. For the east side, the **Brooklyn, Manhattan, Williamsburg,** and **Queensboro bridges,** as well as the **Queens Midtown Tunnel,** cross the East River from Queens and Brooklyn.

Once you arrive in Manhattan, park your car in a garage (expect to pay $20–$45 per day) and leave it there. You really don't need your car for traveling within the city (in fact, it can be more of a hindrance to drive it around the city, especially during rush hours).

By Train
Amtrak (☎ 800/USA-RAIL; www. amtrak.com; book early—as much as 6 months in advance—and travel on weekends for best rates) runs frequent service to New York City's **Penn Station,** on Seventh Avenue between 31st and 33rd streets, as do **New Jersey Transit** and **Long Island Railroad. Metro-North Railroad** runs out of **Grand Central Station** (p 7). You can easily pick up a taxi, subway, or bus to your hotel from either station.

Getting **Around**

By Subway
Run by the **Metropolitan Transit Authority (MTA),** the subway system is the fastest way to travel around New York, especially during rush hours. The subway runs 24 hours a day, 7 days a week. The rush-hour crushes are roughly from 8 to 9:30am and from 5 to 6:30pm on weekdays. The fare is $2.50 (half-price for seniors and those with disabilities) and children under 44 inches tall (111cm) ride free. Fares are paid with a **MetroCard,** a magnetically encoded card that debits the fare when swiped through the turnstile (or the fare box on any city bus). MetroCards also allow you free transfers between the bus and subway within a 2-hour period. There are Pay-Per-Ride and Unlimited-Ride Metro-Cards; both can be purchased at any subway station.

Once you're in town, you can stop at the MTA desk at the **Times Square Information Center,** 1560 Broadway, between 46th and 47th streets (where Broadway meets Seventh Ave.) to pick up the latest subway map. (You can also ask for one at any token booth, but they might not always be available.)

By Bus
Less expensive than taxis, with better views than subways—buses would be the perfect alternative if they didn't sometimes get stuck in traffic. They're best for shorter distances or when you're not in a rush. Like the subway fare, bus fare is $2.50, payable with a **MetroCard** or **exact change.** Bus drivers don't make change, and fare boxes don't accept dollar bills or pennies. If you pay with a MetroCard, you can transfer to another bus or to the subway for free within 2 hours. If you pay cash, you must request a **free transfer** slip that allows you to change to an intersecting bus route only (legal transfer points are listed on the transfer paper) within 1 hour of issue. Transfer slips cannot be used to enter the subway.

By Taxi
Yellow **taxi cabs** are licensed by the Taxi and Limousine Commission (TLC). Base fare on entering the cab is $2.50. The cost is 50¢ for every ⅕ mile or 50¢ per 1 minute in stopped or very slow-moving traffic (or for waiting time); most take credit cards. There's no extra charge for each passenger or for luggage, but you must pay bridge or tunnel tolls. You'll also pay a 50¢ night surcharge after 8pm and before 6am, and a $1 peak-hour surcharge Mon–Fri 4pm–8pm. A 15 to 20 percent tip is customary. You can hail a taxi on any street.

By Bike
In 2013 the city, with funding help from Citi Bank, initiated the **Citi Bike bike-sharing program**

(☎ 855/245-3311; www.citibikenyc. com). Anyone over age 16 can purchase a 24-hour or weekly pass, which gives you access to any bike at the 300 stations throughout the city for unlimited 30-minute trips

(there are overtime fees if you don't dock a bike within 30 minutes). Payment is made with a credit or debit card, and riders are given a code to enter on a keypad that unlocks the bike for use.

Fast **Facts**

APARTMENT RENTALS For month or longer stays, your best bets are **Manhattan Getaways** (☎ 212/ 956-2010; www.manhattan getaways.com) with a network of unhosted apartments around the city that start at $125 per night; **City Sonnet** (www.citysonnet. com; $125–$700 double) for both hosted and unhosted lodging in apartments; or **Manhattan Lodgings** (☎ 212/677-7616; www. manhattanlodgings.com) for B&B and apartment stays.

ATMS (CASHPOINTS) You'll find **automated teller machines (ATMs)** on just about every block in Manhattan, most of which charge a fee to withdraw if you are not a customer of the bank (usually $3, not including any fees your home bank may charge). Some ATMs will allow you to draw U.S. currency against your bank and credit cards. Check with your bank before leaving home and remember that you will need your personal identification number (PIN) to do so.

BABYSITTING The first place to check is with your hotel. Many hotels have babysitting services or will provide you with lists of reliable sitters. If this doesn't pan out, call the **Babysitters' Guild** (☎ 212/682-0227; www. babysittersguild.com). The sitters are licensed, insured, and bonded and can even take your child on outings.

BANKING HOURS Banks tend to be open Monday through Friday from 9am to 6pm and Saturday mornings.

BUSINESS HOURS The city that never sleeps truly doesn't. Most stores stay open until 7pm or later, with drugstores and groceries usually going strong until 9pm, and delis and corner produce markets lasting into the wee hours. Most sstores (except for Midtown and Upper East Side boutiques) are open on Sunday, although they may not open until 11am or noon.

CONSULATES & EMBASSIES All embassies are located in Washington, D.C., although New York has a consulate for virtually every country, and most nations have a mission to the United Nations (also in New York). Call for directory information in Washington, D.C. (☎ 202/555-1212), for the number of your national embassy. The consulate of **Australia** is at 150 E. 42nd St., 34th floor (☎ 212/351-6500). The consulate of **New Zealand** is at 222 E. 41st St., Ste. 2510 (☎ 212/832-4038; www.nzembassy.com). The consulate of **Canada** is at 1251 Ave. of Americas (☎ 212/596-1628; www.canadianembassy.org). The consulate of **Ireland** is at 345 Park Ave., 17th floor (☎ 212/319-2555; www.irelandemb.org). The consulate of the **United Kingdom** is at 845 Third Ave. (☎ 212/745-0200; www.britainusa.com).

CREDIT CARDS Credit cards are a safe way to "carry" money, they provide a convenient record of all your expenses, and they generally offer good exchange rates. You can also withdraw cash advances from your credit cards at banks or ATMs by using a predesignated PIN (see "ATMs [Cashpoints]," above).

DENTISTS If you have dental problems, a nationwide referral service known as **1-800-DENTIST** (☎ 800/336-8478) will provide the name of a nearby dentist or clinic.

DINING With a few exceptions at the high end of the scale, dining attire is fairly casual. It's a good idea to make reservations in advance if you plan to dine between 7 and 9pm.

DOCTORS The **NYU Downtown Hospital** offers physician referrals (☎ 888/698-3362).

ELECTRICITY Like Canada, the U.S. uses 110 to 120 volts AC (60 cycles), compared to 220 to 240 volts AC (50 cycles) in most of Europe, Australia, and New Zealand. If your small appliances use 220 to 240 volts, you'll need a 110-volt transformer and a plug adapter with two flat parallel pins to operate them here. Downward converters that change 220–240 volts to 110–120 volts are difficult to find in the U.S., so bring one with you.

EMERGENCIES Dial ☎ **911** for fire, police, and ambulance. The **Poison Control Center** can be reached at ☎ 800/222-1222 toll-free from any phone. If you encounter serious problems, contact **Traveler's Aid International** (☎ 202/546-1127; www.travelersaid.org) to help direct you to a local branch. This nationwide, nonprofit, social-service organization geared to helping travelers in difficult straits offers services that might include reuniting families separated while traveling, providing food and/or shelter to people stranded without cash, or even offering emotional counseling.

EVENTS LISTINGS Good sources include the **New York Times** (www.nytimes.com) with excellent arts and entertainment coverage, **Time Out New York** (www.timeout.com/newyork) with extensive weekly listings, and the weekly **New York** magazine (www.nymag.com), a great resource for restaurants, art, and cultural events.

FAMILY TRAVEL The best bet for timely information is **Time Out New York Kids** (www.timeout.com/new-york-kids). Another good resource is the "Weekend" section of Friday's **New York Times,** which has a "Spare Times" section dedicated to the week's best kid-friendly activities.

GAY & LESBIAN TRAVELERS All over Manhattan, but especially in such neighborhoods as the **West Village** and **Chelsea,** shops, services, and restaurants cater to a gay and lesbian clientele. The **Lesbian, Gay, Bisexual & Transgender Community Center** is at 208 W. 13th St., between Seventh and Eighth avenues (☎ 212/620-7310; www.gay-center.org).

HOLIDAYS Banks, government offices, post offices, and many stores, restaurants, and museums are closed on the following legal national holidays: January 1 (New Year's Day), the third Monday in January (Martin Luther King, Jr., Day), the third Monday in February (Presidents' Day, Washington's Birthday), the last Monday in May (Memorial Day), July 4 (Independence Day), the first Monday in September (Labor Day), the second Monday in October (Columbus Day), November 11 (Veterans' Day), the fourth Thursday in November (Thanksgiving Day), and December 25 (Christmas). Also, the Tuesday following the first Monday in November is Election Day and is a federal government holiday in presidential-election years (held every 4 years, and next in 2016).

INSURANCE **Trip-cancellation insurance** helps you get your money back if you have to back out of a trip, if you have to go home early, or if your travel supplier goes bankrupt. Also, although it's not required of travelers, **health insurance** is highly recommended. The U.S. does not usually offer free or low-cost medical care to its citizens or visitors. Although lack of health insurance may prevent you from being admitted to a hospital in nonemergencies, don't worry about being left on a street corner to die: The American way is to fix you now and bill the living daylights out of you later.

Lost-luggage insurance is usually provided on domestic flights: Checked baggage is covered up to $2,500 per ticketed passenger. On international flights (including U.S. portions of international trips), baggage is limited to approximately $9 per pound, up to approximately $635 per checked bag.

INTERNET CENTERS The **Times Square Visitor Information Center,** 1560 Broadway, between 46th and 47th streets (☎ 212/768-1560; daily 7am–7pm), has computer terminals that you can use to send e-mails courtesy of Yahoo!. Most hotels and many coffee shops have complimentary Wi-Fi access in their public spaces.

LOST PROPERTY **Travelers Aid** (www.travelersaid.org) helps distressed travelers with all kinds of problems, including lost or stolen luggage. There are locations at **JFK Airport** (☎ 718/656-4870) and in **Newark Airport** (☎ 973/623-5052).

MAIL & POSTAGE The main post office is at 421 Eighth Ave. (at 33rd St.); other branches can be found by calling ☎ 800/275-8777 or logging onto **www.usps.gov**. Mail can be sent to you, in your name, c/o General Delivery at the main post office. Most post offices will hold your mail for up to 1 month and are open Monday to Friday from 8am to 6pm and Saturday from 9am to 3pm. At press time, domestic postage rates were 33¢ for a postcard and 46¢ for a letter. For international mail, a first-class letter of up to 1 ounce costs $1.10.

MONEY Most businesses and restaurants take plastic, and if they don't, there's an ATM or bank on just about every street corner. (Even cabs take credit cards.)

PASSPORTS Keep a photocopy of your passport with you when you're traveling. If your passport is lost or stolen, having a copy will significantly speed up the reissuing process at your consulate (p 170). Keep your passport and other valuables in your room's safe or in the hotel safe.

PHARMACIES **Duane Reade** (www.duanereade.com) has 24-hour pharmacies in **Midtown** at 224 W. 57th St., at Broadway (☎ 212/541-9708); on the **Upper West Side** at 253 W. 72nd St., between Broadway and West End Avenue (☎ 212/580-0497); and on the **Upper East Side** at 1279 Third Ave., at 74th Street (☎ 212/744-2668), as well as other locations. **CVS** (www.cvs.com) also has 24-hour pharmacies around the city.

SAFETY New York is one of the safest large cities in the U.S. But that doesn't mean you should take a stroll through Central Park in the wee hours of the morning, leave unsecured valuables in your car, or flash wads of cash in Times Square. No, no, and no. Avoid being the victim of petty crime by using common sense: Store your wallet in a safe place; wear your purse so it's not snatchable (although you don't have to wear your backpack on your front—that's just silly); lock up any valuables in the hotel safe; and avoid low-trafficked areas, especially at night. The NYPD has a comprehensive **Crime Prevention**

Tips list on the NYC.gov website (www.nyc.gov/html/nypd).

SENIOR TRAVELERS New York subway and bus fares are half-price ($1) for people 65 and older. Many museums and sights (and some theaters and performance halls) offer discounted admission and tickets to seniors, so don't be shy about asking and always bring an ID card. Members of **AARP** (☎ 888/687-2277 or 202/434-2277; www.aarp.org) get discounts on hotels, airfares, and car rentals. Anyone 50 or over can join.

SMOKING Smoking is prohibited on public transportation, in hotel and office-building lobbies, in taxis, in bars and restaurants, and in most shops.

SPECTATOR SPORTS You've got your choice of baseball teams: the **Yankees** (☎ 718/293-6000; www.yankees.com) or the **Mets** (☎ 718/507-TIXX; www.mets.com). For basketball, there's the **Knicks** (☎ 877/NYK-DUNK; www.nyknicks.com) and the **New York Liberty** (☎ 212/564-9622; www.wnba.com/liberty). The **New York Giants** (☎ 201/935-8222; www.giants.com) and **Jets** (☎ 800/469-JETS; www.newyorkjets.com) cover your football options.

TAXES **Sales tax** is 8.875 percent on meals, most goods, and some services. **Hotel tax** is 14.75 percent plus $3.50 per room per night (including sales tax). **Parking garage tax** is 18.375 percent (residents get a reduced rate).

TELEPHONE For directory assistance, dial ☎ 411; for long-distance information, dial 1, then the appropriate area code and 555-1212. Pay phones cost 25¢ or 50¢ for local calls. There are four area codes in the city: two in Manhattan, the original **212** and the newer **646**, and two in the outer boroughs, the original **718** and the newer **347**. The **917** area code is

assigned to cellphones, pagers, and the like. Calls between these area codes are local, but you'll have to dial the area code plus the seven digits, even within your area code.

TICKETS Tickets for concerts at all larger theaters can be purchased through **Ticketmaster** (☎ 212/307-7171; www.ticketmaster.com). For advance tickets at smaller venues, contact **Ticketweb** (☎ 866/468-7619; www.ticketweb.com). You can buy theater tickets in advance from **TeleCharge** (☎ 212/239-6200; www.telecharge.com) or **Ticketmaster** (☎ 212/307-4100; www.ticketmaster.com). If you want last-minute tickets, see p 147.

TIPPING In hotels, tip **bellhops** at least $1 per bag ($2–$3 if you have a lot of luggage) and tip the **chamber staff** $1 to $2 per day (more if you've left a disaster area for him or her to clean up, or if you're traveling with messy kids and/or pets). Tip the **doorman** or **concierge** only if he or she has provided you with some specific service (such as calling a cab). In restaurants, bars, and nightclubs, tip **service staff** 15 to 20 percent of the check, tip **bartenders** 10 to 15 percent, and tip **checkroom attendants** $1 per garment. Tipping is not expected in cafeterias and fast-food restaurants. Tip **cab drivers** 15 to 20 percent of the fare and tip **skycaps** at airports at least $1 per bag ($2–$3 if you have a lot of luggage).

TOILETS Public restrooms are available at the **visitor centers** in Midtown (1560 Broadway, btw. 46th & 47th sts.; and 810 Seventh Ave., btw. 52nd & 53rd sts.). Grand Central Terminal, at 42nd Street between Park and Lexington avenues, and the High Line entrance at 16th Street and Tenth Avenue also have clean restrooms. Your best bet on the street is **Starbucks** or another city java chain—you can't walk more than a few blocks without seeing one. The big **chain bookstores** are good for this, too. On the Lower East Side, stop into the **Lower East Side Visitor Center,** 54 Orchard St., between Hester and Grand streets (Mon–Fri 9:30am–5:30pm, Sat–Sun 9:30am–4pm).

TOURIST OFFICES   NYC & Company is the city's official marketing and tourism organization, located at 810 Seventh Ave., New York, NY 10019 (☎ 212/484-1200; www. nycgo.com).

TOURS   Scholar-led private or group walking tours with award-winning tour operator **Context Travel** (☎ 800/691-6036; www.context-travel.com) offer in-depth looks at the city's art, architecture, and urban history. **Big Apple Greeter** (☎ 212/669-8159; www.bigapplegreeter.org) provides free neighborhood walking tours. Or try one of the hop-on, hop-off double-decker bus tours offered by **Gray Line** (☎ 800/669-0051; www.graylinenewyork.com).

TRAVELERS WITH DISABILITIES   Hospital Audiences, Inc. (☎ 212/575-7676; www.hospitalaudiences.org) arranges attendance and provides details about accessibility at cultural institutions as well as cultural events adapted for people with disabilities. Services include the invaluable **HAI Hot Line** (☎ 212/575-7676), which offers accessibility information for hotels, restaurants, attractions, cultural venues, and

much more. This nonprofit organization also publishes *Access for All,* a guidebook on accessibility, available free of charge on the Hospital Audiences website. Another terrific source for travelers with disabilities who are coming to New York City is **Big Apple Greeter** (☎ 212/669-8159; www.bigapplegreeter.org). Its employees are well versed in accessibility issues. They can provide a resource list of agencies that serve the city's community with disabilities, and sometimes have special discounts available for theater and music performances. Big Apple Greeter even offers one-to-one tours that pair volunteers with visitors with disabilities; they can also introduce you to the public transportation system. Reserve at least 1 week ahead.

   Public buses are an inexpensive and easy way to get around New York. All buses' back doors are supposed to be equipped with wheelchair lifts. Buses also "kneel," lowering their front steps for people who have difficulty boarding. Passengers with disabilities pay half-price fares ($1). The **subway** isn't yet fully wheelchair accessible, but a list of about 30 accessible subway stations and a guide to wheelchair-accessible subway itineraries are on the MTA website. Call ☎ **718/596-8585** for bus and subway transit info or go online to **www.mta.nyc.ny.us/nyct** and click on the wheelchair symbol.

A Brief **History of New York**

1664 The Dutch surrender New Amsterdam to the British, and the island is renamed after the brother of King Charles II, the Duke of York.

1765 The Sons of Liberty burn the British governor in effigy.

1776 Independence from England is declared.

1789 The first Congress is held at Federal Hall on Wall Street, and George Washington is inaugurated.

1792 The first stock exchange is established on Wall Street.

1820 New York City is the nation's largest city, with a population of 124,000.

1863 The draft riots rage throughout New York; 125 people die, including 11 African Americans who are lynched by mobs of Irish immigrants.

1883 The Brooklyn Bridge opens.

1886 The Statue of Liberty is completed.

1892 Ellis Island opens and begins processing more than a million immigrants a year.

1904 The first subway departs from City Hall.

1920 Babe Ruth joins the New York Yankees.

1929 The stock market crashes.

1931 The Empire State Building opens and is the tallest building in the world.

1939 The New York World's Fair opens in Flushing Meadows, Queens.

1947 The Brooklyn Dodgers sign Jackie Robinson, the first African American to play in the Major Leagues.

1957 Elvis Presley performs live in New York on *The Ed Sullivan Show*.

1969 The Gay Rights movement begins with the Stonewall Rebellion in Greenwich Village. The Amazin' Mets win the World Series.

1990 David Dinkins is elected as the first African-American mayor of New York City.

2000 The New York Yankees beat the New York Mets in the first Subway Series in 44 years. New York's population exceeds eight million.

2001 Terrorists use hijacked planes to crash into the Twin Towers of the World Trade Center, which brings both towers down and kills more than 3,000 people.

2003 Smoking is banned in all restaurants and bars.

2004 Ground breaks on the new One World Trade Center building.

2009 The New York Yankees win the World Series in their first year in the new Yankee Stadium, giving them 27 World Series championships.

2011 Same-sex marriage becomes legal in the state of New York.

2012 Hurricane Sandy, the worst storm to ever hit New York, bears down on the city and inflicts billions of dollars' worth of damage.

New York **Architecture**

New York is famous for its great buildings, but the truth is that the most interesting thing about its architecture is its diversity. From elegant Greek Revival row houses to soaring glass skyscrapers, the city contains examples of just about every style. Constructed over 300 years, these buildings represent the changing tastes of the city's residents from Colonial times to the present.

Georgian (1700–76)

This style reflects Renaissance ideas made popular in England, and later in the U.S., through the publication of books on 16th-century Italian architects. Georgian houses are characterized by a formal arrangement of parts employing a symmetrical composition enriched with classical details, such as columns and pediments.

St. Paul's Chapel (p 15), the only pre-Revolutionary building in Manhattan, is an almost perfect example of the Georgian style, with a pediment, colossal columns, Palladian window, quoins, and balustrade above the roofline.

Federal (1780–1820)

Federal was the first American architectural style. It was an adaptation of a contemporary English style called Adam (after Scottish architects Robert and James Adam), which included ornate, colorful interior decoration. Federal combined Georgian architecture with the delicacy of the French rococo and the classical architecture of Greece and Rome. The overall effect is one of restraint and dignity, which may appear delicate when compared to the more robust Georgian style.

In the **West Village** (p 6), near and along Bedford Street between Christopher and Morton streets, are more original Federal-style houses than anywhere else in Manhattan.

A typical Federal exterior.

House nos. 4 through 10 (built 1834) on Grove Street, just off Bedford, present one of the most authentic groups of late-Federal-style houses in America.

Greek Revival (1820–60)

The Greek Revolution in the 1820s, in which Greece won its independence from the Turks, recalled to American intellectuals the democracy of ancient Greece—and its elegant architecture. At the same time, the War of 1812 diminished American affection for the British influence. With many believing America to be the spiritual successor of Greece, the use of classical Greek forms came to dominate residential, commercial, and government architecture.

Perhaps the city's finest Greek Revival building is **Federal Hall National Memorial** (built 1842; p 63), 26 Wall St., at Nassau Street. The structure has a Greek temple front, with Doric columns and a simple pediment, resting on a high base called a plinth, with a steep flight of steps.

Gothic Revival (1830–60)

The term "Gothic Revival" refers to a literary and aesthetic movement of the 1830s and '40s that occurred in England and the U.S. Adherents believed that the wickedness of modern times could benefit from a dose of "goodness" presumed to have been associated with the Christian medieval past. Architecture was chosen as one of the vehicles to bring this message to the people. Some structures had only one or two Gothic features, while others, usually churches, were copies of English Gothic structures.

Trinity Church (p 17), at Broadway and Wall Street (Richard Upjohn, 1846), is one of the most celebrated Gothic Revival structures in the U.S. Here you see all the features of a Gothic church: a steeple, battlements, pointed arches, Gothic tracery, stained-glass windows, flying buttresses (an external bracing system for supporting a roof or vault), and medieval sculptures.

Italianate (1840–80)

The architecture of Italy served as the inspiration for this building style, which could be as picturesque as the Gothic or as restrained as the classical. In New York, the style was used for urban row houses and commercial buildings. The development of cast iron at this time permitted the inexpensive mass production of decorative features that few could have afforded in carved stone. This led to the creation of cast-iron districts in nearly every American city.

New York's **SoHo Cast Iron Historic District** has 26 blocks jammed with cast-iron facades, many in the Italianate manner. The single richest section is **Greene Street** between Houston and Canal streets.

Early Skyscraper (1880–1920)

The invention of the skyscraper can be traced directly to the use of cast iron in the 1840s for storefronts, such as those seen in SoHo. Experimentation with cast and wrought iron in the construction of interior skeletons eventually allowed buildings to rise higher. These buildings were spacious, cost-effective, efficient, and quickly erected—in short, the perfect architectural solution for America's growing downtowns. But solving the technical problems of the skyscraper did not resolve how the buildings should look. Most solutions relied on historical precedents, including decoration reminiscent of the Gothic, Romanesque (a style characterized by the use of rounded arches), or Beaux Arts.

Examples include the **American Surety Company,** at 100 Broadway (Bruce Price, 1895); the triangular **Flatiron Building** (p 6), at Fifth Avenue and 23rd Street (Daniel H. Burnham & Co., 1902), with strong tripartite divisions and Renaissance Revival detail; and the **Woolworth Building** (Cass Gilbert, 1913; p 15), on Broadway at Park Place.

Second Renaissance Revival (1890–1920)

Buildings in this style show a studied formalism. A relative faithfulness to Italian Renaissance precedents of window and doorway treatments distinguishes it from the looser adaptations of the Italianate. Scale and size, in turn, set the Second Renaissance Revival apart from the first, which occurred from 1840 to 1890. The style was used for banks, swank town houses, government buildings, and private clubs.

New York's Upper East Side has two fine examples of this building type, each exhibiting most of the style's key features: the **Racquet and Tennis Club,** 370 Park Ave. (McKim, Mead & White, 1918), based on the style of an elegant Florentine palazzo; and the **Metropolitan Club,** 1 E. 60th St. (McKim, Mead & White, 1894).

Beaux Arts (1890–1920)

This style takes its name from the Ecole des Beaux-Arts in Paris, where a number of prominent American architects trained, beginning around the mid–19th century. These architects adopted the academic design principles of the Ecole, which emphasized the study of Greek and Roman structures, composition, and symmetry and the creation of elaborate presentation drawings. Because of the idealized origins and grandiose use of classical forms, the Beaux Arts in America was seen as the ideal style for expressing civic pride. Grandiose compositions, an exuberance of detail, and a variety of stone finishes typify most Beaux Arts structures.

The **New York Public Library** (p 8), at Fifth Avenue and 42nd Street (Carrère & Hastings, 1911), is perhaps the best example. Others of note are **Grand Central Terminal** (p 7), at 42nd Street and Park Avenue (Reed & Stem and Warren & Whetmore, 1913), and the **Alexander Hamilton U.S. Custom House** (Cass Gilbert, 1907), on Bowling Green between State and Whitehall streets.

International Style (1920–45)

In 1932, the Museum of Modern Art hosted its first architecture exhibit, titled simply *Modern Architecture*. Displays included images of International Style buildings from around the world.

The structures all share a stark simplicity and vigorous functionalism, a definite break from historically based, decorative styles. The International Style was popularized in the U.S. through the teachings and designs of **Ludwig Mies van der Rohe** (1886–1969), a German émigré based in Chicago. Interpretations of the "Miesian" International Style were built in most U.S. cities as late as 1980.

Two famous examples of this style in New York are the **Seagram Building,** at 375 Park Ave. (Ludwig Mies van der Rohe, 1958), and the **Lever House,** at 390 Park Ave., between 53rd and 54th streets (Skidmore, Owings & Merrill, 1952).

Art Deco (1925–40)

Art Deco is a decorative style that took its name from a Paris exposition in 1925. The jazzy style embodied the idea of modernity. One of the first widely accepted styles not based on historic precedents, it influenced all areas of design from jewelry and household goods to cars, trains, and ocean liners. Art Deco buildings are characterized

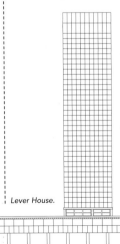

Lever House.

by a linear, hard edge, or angular composition, often with a vertical emphasis and highlighted with stylized decoration.

Despite the effects of the Depression, several major Art Deco structures were built in New York in the 1930s, often providing crucial jobs. **Rockefeller Center** (Raymond Hood, 1940; p 8) includes 30 Rockefeller Plaza, a tour de force of Art Deco style, with a soaring vertical shaft and aluminum details. The **Chrysler Building**'s needlelike spire (William Allen, 1930; p 7), with zigzag patterns in glass and metal is a distinctive feature on the city's skyline. The famous **Empire State Building** (Shreve, Lamb & Harmon, 1931; p 7) contains a black- and silver-toned lobby among its many Art Deco features.

Art Moderne (1930–45)

Art Moderne strove for modernity and an artistic expression for the sleekness of the Machine Age. Unbroken horizontal lines and smooth curves visually distinguish it from Art Deco and give it a streamlined effect. It was popular with movie theaters and was often applied to cars, trains, and boats to suggest the idea of speed.

Radio City Music Hall (p 8), on Sixth Avenue at 50th Street (Edward Durrell Stone and Donald Deskey, 1932), has a sweeping Art Moderne marquee.

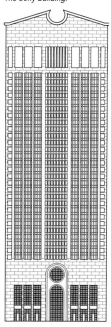

The Sony Building.

Postmodern (1975–90)

Postmodernism burst on the scene in the 1970s with the reintroduction of historical precedents in architecture. With many feeling that the office towers of the previous style were too cold, postmodernists began to incorporate classical details and recognizable forms into their designs—often applied in outrageous proportions.

The **Sony Building,** at 550 Madison Ave. (Philip Johnson/John Burgee, 1984), brings the distinctive shape of a Chippendale cabinet to the New York skyline.

The Chrysler Building.

Index

See also Accommodations and Restaurant indexes, below.

Numbers

A

B

Photo **Credits**

p i, left: @ vvoe / Shutterstock.com; p i, middle: @ cristapper.Shutterstock.com; p i, right: @ SeanPavonePhoto / Shutterstock.com; p viii; @ Shayna Marchese; p 3, bottom: Courtesy of Jade Bar; p 4, bottom: @ Shayna Marchese; p 5: @ Shayna Marchese; p 7, bottom: @ Shayna Marchese; p 8, bottom: @ Ellinor Stigle; p 9, top: @ Erik Rank; p 11, bottom: @ Audrey Kang; p 12, bottom: @ Alden Gewirtz; p 13, top: @ Alden Gewirtz; p 16, bottom: @ screenpunk; p 17, top: @ Michael Mohr; p 18, bottom: @ Paskee / Shutterstock.com; p 19: @ Audrey Kang; p 21, bottom: @ Ellinor Stigle; p 22, bottom: @ Seth Olenick; p 23, top: @ Michael Mohr; p 25, bottom: @ Shayna Marchese; p 26, top: Courtesy of The Frick Collection, photo by Michael Bodycomb; p 26, bottom: @ Northfotov/Shutterstock.com; p 27, top: @ Ellinor Stigle; p 27, bottom: @ Cherie Cincilla; p 30, bottom: @ eddtoro / Shutterstock.com; p 31, top: @ Keith Sherwood / Shutterstock.com; p 33, bottom: @ Ellinor Stigle; p 34, top: @ littleny / Shutterstock.com; p 35, top: @ Ellinor Stigle; p 35, bottom: @ Cherie Cincilla; p 37, bottom: @ Andreas Juergensmeier; p 38, top: @ Alden Gewirtz; p 39, top: @ Shayna Marchese; p 39, bottom: @ Shayna Marchese; p 41, top: @ Alden Gewirtz; p 41, bottom: @ stockelements; p 43, top: Courtesy of New York Philharmonic / Photo by Chris Lee; p 43, bottom: @ Andreas Juergensmeier; p 44, top: @ Cherie Cincilla; p 45: @ Erik Rank; p 47, top: @ Audrey Kang; p 49, top: @ Audrey Kang; p 51, bottom: @ saitowitz; p 53, bottom: @ Alden Gewirtz; p 57, top: @ Erik Rank; p 59: @ Christy Havranek; p 61, top: @ Stuart Monk / Shutterstock.com; p 62, top: @ Shayna Marchese; p 65, top: @ Seth Olenick; p 66, bottom: @ Shayna M̶̶̶

@ Christy Havranek; p 71, top: @ Al̶̶
Courtesy of Gagosian Gallery, Phot̶̶̶̶̶̶̶̶̶̶̶̶̶̶̶̶̶̶̶̶̶̶̶̶̶̶̶̶̶̶̶̶̶̶̶̶̶̶
Havranek; p 75, bottom: @ Christy ̶̶
@ Alden Gewirtz; p 79, top: @ Alde̶̶̶̶̶̶̶̶̶̶̶̶̶̶̶̶̶̶̶̶̶̶̶̶̶̶̶̶̶̶̶̶̶̶̶̶̶̶

Photo by Adam Husted; p 82, bott̶̶̶̶̶̶̶̶̶̶̶̶̶̶̶̶̶̶̶̶̶̶̶̶̶̶̶̶̶̶̶̶̶̶̶̶̶̶
@ Elzbieta Sekowska / Shutterstock̶̶̶̶̶̶̶̶̶̶̶̶̶̶̶̶̶̶̶̶̶̶̶̶̶̶̶̶̶̶̶̶̶̶
@ Ellinor Stigle; p 86, top: @ Andre̶̶̶̶̶̶̶̶̶̶̶̶̶̶̶̶̶̶̶̶̶̶̶̶̶̶̶̶̶̶̶̶̶̶̶̶
p 87, bottom: @ Audrey Kang; p 8̶̶
bottom: @ Christy Havranek; p 95, ̶̶
p 96, bottom: @ Cherie Cincilla; p ̶̶

Gewirtz; p 98, bottom: @ Alden G̶̶
@ Alden Gewirtz; p 101, bottom: @̶̶
Cincilla; p 105, bottom: @ Alden G̶̶̶̶̶̶̶̶̶̶̶̶̶̶̶̶̶̶̶̶̶̶̶̶̶̶̶̶̶̶̶̶̶̶̶̶̶̶
@ Alden Gewirtz; p 109, bottom: @̶̶
p 111: @ Michael Mohr; p 116, bot̶̶̶̶̶̶̶̶̶̶̶̶̶̶̶̶̶̶̶̶̶̶̶̶̶̶̶̶̶̶̶̶̶̶̶̶̶̶
bottom: @ Christy Havranek; p 11̶̶
Havranek; p 120, top: @ Christy H̶̶̶̶̶̶̶̶̶̶̶̶̶̶̶̶̶̶̶̶̶̶̶̶̶̶̶̶̶̶̶̶̶̶̶̶̶̶
@ Erik Rank; p 122, top: @ Rosapo̶̶̶̶̶̶̶̶̶̶̶̶̶̶̶̶̶̶̶̶̶̶̶̶̶̶̶̶̶̶̶̶̶̶̶̶
Robertson; p 125: @ Christy Havra̶̶̶̶̶̶̶̶̶̶̶̶̶̶̶̶̶̶̶̶̶̶̶̶̶̶̶̶̶̶̶̶̶̶̶̶
bottom: Courtesy of Bowlmor Lan̶̶̶̶̶̶̶̶̶̶̶̶̶̶̶̶̶̶̶̶̶̶̶̶̶̶̶̶̶̶̶̶̶̶̶̶
of The Jane; p 133, bottom: @ Ch̶̶
tesy of Caroline's; p 141, bottom: @ Smoke Jazz & Supper Club; p ̶̶̶̶̶̶̶̶̶̶̶̶̶̶̶̶̶̶̶̶̶̶̶̶̶̶̶̶̶̶
Jazz at Lincoln Center, photo by Elizabeth Leitzell; p 143, top: Courtesy of 92nd Street Y; p 144, bottom: @ Shayna Marchese; p 145, top: @ Michael Mohr; p 146, top: @ SeanPavonePhoto/Shutterstock.com; p 146, bottom: @ Sydney Lowe; p 149: Courtesy of Firmdale Hotels; p 154, top: Courtesy of Ace Hotel; p 155, bottom: Courtesy of Andaz Wall Street; p 156, top: @ Alden Gewirtz; p 156, bottom: Courtesy of Gild Hall; p 157, top: @ Alden Gewirtz; p 158, top: Courtesy of The Jane; p 158, bottom: Courtesy of Le Parker-Meridien; p 159, bottom: Courtesy of The Peninsula; p 160, top: Courtesy of Ritz Carlton; p 160, bottom: Courtesy of Sofitel Hotel; p 162, bottom: Courtesy of Washington Square Hotel; p 163: @ Stuart Monk / Shutterstock.com